Neil Perry AM is Australia's leading and most influential chef. He has managed several quality restaurants in Australia and today concentrates on his flagship brand, the Rockpool Group, which includes Rockpool est. 1989; Rockpool Bar & Grill Sydney, Melbourne and Perth; Spice Temple Sydney and Melbourne; Rosetta Ristorante, Melbourne; and the recently opened Burger Project in Sydney's World Square. He also heads a team of seven consultants to Qantas, developing quarterly menus for First and Business travellers and Qantas Lounges. Neil is a television presenter, with regular appearances as a judge on *MasterChef Australia* and his own show on *The Lifestyle Channel*, and has a weekly food column in *Good Weekend* in *the Sydney Morning Herald* and *The Age,* as well as contributing a monthly food column to *Qantas: The Australian Way* magazine and *Good Food*. He is also the author of eight cookbooks: *Good Food, The Food I Love, Rockpool, Simply Asian, Balance & Harmony, Rockpool Bar & Grill, Easy Weekends* and *Simply Good Food*.

*To Andy Evans and Ben Pollard, two fabulous cooks
who have come on my Chinese journey with me, and
have grown into two wonderful men I'm very proud of.*

SPICE TEMPLE

NEIL PERRY

Photography by Earl Carter

LANTERN

an imprint of
PENGUIN BOOKS

CONTENTS

INTRODUCTION

My love of Chinese food – first eating it, and then cooking it – goes back to my earliest memories of my father. Memories of him and me walking through Chinatown, buying mysterious things in shops filled with the musty smell of dried ingredients that he would later bring to life in his cooking. And memories of family meals at various restaurants: I still remember the climb up the stairs at the Mandarin on George Street, the Old Tai Yuen, or perhaps the Dixon, and later the Shanghai Village – all these places where Dad knew the staff and could get us food far removed from the sweet and sour pork, chicken chow mein or beef in black bean sauce that were so popular in the sixties in Sydney. Dad's friends from these restaurants invited us into their homes, and we went to wedding banquets and other family gatherings, where I encountered great Chinese cooking. As a boy, I not only found this food amazing to look at, but I also fell in love with the taste, the variety and the textures. Looking back, who wouldn't love crispy-skin chicken, roast glistening-skin duck, red-braised pork shoulder, chilli mud crab, abalone soup and steamed fish with ginger and spring onion? But I also learnt what a great way to eat shared plates are, and how they change the dining dynamic. These early experiences have guided my life way beyond anything I could possibly have imagined.

Fast forward to 1984. I'd been cooking professionally for just a year, and was lucky enough to be made head chef at Barrenjoey House Restaurant, Palm Beach. With Damien and Josephine Pignolet, Stephanie Alexander, Jenny Ferguson, and Gay and Tony Bilson as my mentors, the food I was cooking was essentially French provincial. Fascinated by the French Michelin three-star chefs whose focus and obsessive attention to detail I was reading so much about, I travelled to France, Switzerland and Italy, taking in more than a dozen three-Michelin-starred restaurants in 21 days . . . and putting on about five kilos of extra girth by the finish!

On my return, it gradually dawned on me that perhaps it didn't make as much sense for an Australian to be cooking French food in Sydney as it did for the French guys to be doing it in France. It was a simple observation, but one that changed my life as a chef forever. From that time on, I decided that I would incorporate into my style of cooking all the things I love to eat and all the cultures that make Australia the place it is.

As my cooking evolved and Rockpool opened its doors in 1989, I was increasingly looking towards the cultures and food I loved most – and that was Chinese. I started to create dishes with Chinese ingredients and using Chinese techniques, but by changing their nature while respecting their heritage, I made them my own. By 1994, we were putting so many Asian dishes on the menu that we decided we needed a restaurant where we could cook all the Chinese, Thai and Vietnamese food we loved. That place was Wockpool, Potts Point, and I put a fine young cook called Kylie Kwong in charge of the kitchen.

The sub-basement that became a restaurant

When we called time on Wockpool in 2005, to concentrate on opening Rockpool Bar & Grill in Melbourne, Asian food was moved to the back burner for a time. But then, in 2007, while we were searching for a site for Rockpool Bar & Grill in Sydney, a magical thing happened: we found the perfect space for a restaurant I'd been hatching ever since Wockpool closed its doors. I wanted to do something different, a pure Chinese restaurant – but not anything I had done before, so that ruled out a lot of Cantonese food. It was then that I realised it had to be regional. After all, with 22 provinces and several autonomous and special administrative regions, all with their own distinct food traditions, I was bound to find plenty of varied and interesting dishes from this vast country. And so the idea for my beautiful Spice Temple was born.

That first Spice Temple in Sydney was all about fate. When my business partners, Dave Doyle and Trish Richards, and I were weighing up premises in Hunter Street that would eventually become Rockpool Bar & Grill, the deal breaker was whether we would be able to install adequate extraction for a commercial kitchen. In a heritage building with walls of marble or stucco, siting any external vents was problematic. However, the sub-basement had been a club called Pickwick's in a previous life and, as luck would have it, their disused kitchen included an internal ventilation shaft that went all the way up to the eleventh floor. As we made our way down a dimly lit set of concrete stairs into the cavernous subbasement, our vision for Rockpool Bar & Grill Sydney came to life again.

But another thing struck me as well. The dungeon-like space would be perfect for the Chinese restaurant I had in mind. We didn't need daylight and we didn't need magnificent high ceilings and marble like we had upstairs. What we needed was a space where we could control the light to create a sultry atmosphere around spicy food – almost raw in nature, this would be the exact opposite of the refined restaurant we were creating upstairs. It didn't take long for Trish and Dave to see the possibilities of the space, and so Spice Temple Sydney took flight. Quite literally, as I set off on a trip that would help to define Spice Temple.

China: one week, 28 meals, 280 dishes

In May 2008 I landed in Hong Kong and met up with Andy Evans, who had by then been appointed Spice Temple head chef, my assistant Sarah Swan, and Rob McKeown. A Chinese-speaker and food expert, Rob was going to show us around. Our mission was two lunches and two dinners a day, plus various snacks, noodles, congees and sweets in between. We never felt hungry from the moment we arrived to the moment we left Hong Kong.

We spent a couple of days in Hong Kong, a couple in Shanghai and three days in Beijing. In each city we tried lots of different regional foods, eating at places ranging from upmarket restaurant to real local joints. Each meal would comprise about ten dishes, and we would taste, take notes, photograph and dissect each dish, filing away lots of information and taste memories. In Beijing we also ate at the restaurants and cafes inside the government offices that represent each province, sampling authentic foods from Hunan, Yunnan, Sichuan, Xinjiang, Jiangxi and Guangxi. By the end of that week, we had eaten incredibly well, and discovered some wonderful classic dishes from China's regions.

I came back to Sydney with about 150 dishes that could easily have made it onto the menu, but I had decided we would start with no more than 70. I kept whittling it down and down, trying to get the right balance of dishes, ones that represented a number of different provinces. In the end Andy and I tested about 90-odd dishes in a month. We then retested everything that would be on the menu twice more: recipes, photos and plates chosen. Next we cooked them all again for Dave to try, and we tasted wines with them. With a short wine list, it was important that every single wine on the list went perfectly with the food. Linden Pride came on board as our bar manager, creating a cocktail list focused on fresh fruit and natural sodas, and inspired by the 12 Chinese zodiac signs.

Spice Temple Sydney opened in January 2009, and Melbourne followed in late 2010. The rest, as they say, is history.

THE STORIES
BEHIND SPICE TEMPLE

Josephine Perry

I remember the opening night of Spice Temple like it was yesterday. I was young, very young. Fourteen and a half, to be exact. It was an absolute nightmare – one I was sure my dad had been having for weeks! The builders were still there at 5.30 p.m., the floor and the kitchen were nowhere near ready, we had no liquor licence, and Dad was the most stressed I'd ever seen him. A few weeks earlier, I had asked if I could help on opening night, and I was excited to be there. But I was also a young, awkward teenage girl, and when the time came I found myself refusing to put on the uniform. It was a black, figure-hugging, Asian-inspired dress, and I was embarrassed. When Dad raised his voice at me for the first time in my life, I knew he was serious, and I was scared. I began to cry and I left. Outside, I called my mum, who told me to jump in a cab and come home. Once I got there, she settled me down, before telling me I was being ridiculous: 'Dad does so much for you, you can do this for Dad.' She drove me back to Spice Temple, I put on my dress and I worked the night from start to finish. The pride on my dad's face was worth every second of my teenage angst – and although I never would have admitted it at the time, I actually enjoyed myself.

When the dust had settled from opening night, I asked if I could have a job. As I was still at school, I started out doing Friday and Saturday nights. I was under-age and couldn't serve alcohol, which meant I was limited to running food and polishing, but eventually I got taught how to run the pass, and I loved it! Being relied on by my team made me feel important, but it also came with great responsibility, and I had to mature fast. It wasn't without its challenges: I was working with people who were between 10 and 30 years older than me and had years of hospitality experience; I was missing out on friends' parties on the weekends; and there was always this 'Am I only here because of my dad?' voice in my head. I tried to introduce myself as Josephine to new staff, and would hide the fact I was Neil Perry's daughter for as long as I could. Not because I was embarrassed or ashamed, but because I wanted to feel like I could have worked there whether he was my father or not.

Working with Andy Evans has been one of the most valuable experiences of my life. The combination of Andy and Spice Temple changed my whole perspective on eating. I was a very difficult child when it came to food. I wouldn't eat fruit, I wouldn't eat vegetables, and no matter how small Dad tried to dice or julienne them, I would sit at the table for as long as it took to pick all the things I didn't want out of my dinner before I started.

As Andy started at Rockpool in 1994, the year I was born, I'd grown up with him, and I trusted and admired him greatly. If he asked me to taste something, I'd taste it . . . and often I'd like it. He constantly challenged me, and this encouraged me to challenge myself. I now happily dine at three-Michelin-starred restaurants and have an extremely large appetite – which I claim is just making up for lost time. Andy, I'm forever indebted to you. I wouldn't be able to travel the world and do all the things I do, if you hadn't held me down and forced me to eat weird shit! You're like a brother to me, and I love you.

Baci, I still can't believe you took me on. You taught me to be strong, to be confident, and to take responsibility. To always be honest, no matter how big the mistake was. You were tough on me, but I wouldn't have been able to get to where I am now if you hadn't pulled me into line. I can't thank you enough for genuinely wanting to see me succeed, and wanting the best for me. You made me feel like I was an important part of your team and that I belonged.

Dad, where do I even start? I still think back to the day I told you I wanted to leave school and work for you – one of the most daunting days of my life. You supported me beyond all the scenarios I'd been playing out in my head. Your love, support, generosity and kindness are infectious, and are the things that have gotten me so far at such a young age; you have such a nurturing spirit. You're also the most passionate person I have ever met, and the way you inspire others inspires me. You're a role model to me, I look up to you and I adore you. Thank you for everything.

To Spice Temple, thank you for luring me into this crazy yet wonderful life!

Andy Evans

Head Chef, Spice Temple Sydney

Spice Temple opened its doors on 9 January 2009, my daughter's first birthday. I remember being in the park, sitting on the swings and thinking about cupcakes, and also how to roast and grind Sichuan pepper properly.

Since starting at Rockpool in 1994, I had been completely enthralled by the mysteries of Asian cuisine. In one my first few weeks at Rockpool, when chef Mike McEnearney gave me the head of a crispy pigeon with lime and Sichuan salt to munch on, I thought the guy was nuts. By no means an adventurous eater, I was very nervous, but he reassured me that he would never give anyone something they couldn't eat. So, with some judicious seasoning, I popped it in my mouth and had my moment – the one so many chefs have, when they realise that greater powers are in force when you feed someone. The ability to transform someone's preconceptions is a powerful tool, and in the right hands, magic happens. I became addicted to the exotic, and surrounded myself with every weird ingredient I could find. Breaking into another world can be very daunting, and my daily trips to Chinatown were a huge learning curve. However, Neil has been a generous guide, and a firm believer in Asian food's powers of seduction. He has always been a chef who will drop everything to share his passion and knowledge, if you show you are keen.

Travelling to China in 2008 with Neil, Sarah and Rob was like starting all over again, as regional Chinese food I had never really understood became the focus and ultimately the bones of Spice Temple. The basis of good Chinese cooking is balance, and to achieve this we have dishes on the menu from many regions. Over the first few days, Baci, Christian, Brendan, Neil and myself would bicker over the sequence of service, the proper pronunciation of the names of regions, and how to impress on everyone what an enormous challenge we were undertaking. Like the fine professionals they are, they rose to the challenge (with many tears and much wine) and broke the restaurant in, taming the crazy horse that is Spice Temple.

The process of actually getting a dish from idea to restaurant menu may seem quite straightforward, but in reality it is a painfully humbling experience. One dish may be cooked as many as a dozen or more times in many, many ways (and with much grumbling) before it makes it anywhere near diners. Ingredients you thought would work together turn out to be complete garbage, and it is only through constant testing and tasting that we refine each dish to the point where we're finally happy with the result. To put it into perspective, one dish per week over the six years Spice Temple has been open, remade say a half a dozen times, equates to roughly 1872 dishes, most of them failures. Such a large number of failures serves as an indication that each dish on the menu must have a purpose, and will balance and complement the rest of the menu. Life without balance is just shit. This has been the mantra that Neil has made us live by.

When Neil generously offered the job of head chef to me, it made me feel very proud. To be asked by the big guy to head anything is an extraordinary opportunity. I love the fact that Spice Temple can still be a challenge for both customers and staff. It keeps us on our toes, but with countless hours of hard work and training under our belts, it's fantastic to see it in full swing. To see people enjoying themselves puts a glow even into the most hardened of hearts. There are times when we don't get it right, and they hurt. But when we do, it is my favourite place in the world to eat. The enthusiasm, dedication and style the staff delivers is a wonderful thing to be a part of.

As this was my first head chef position, it would be insulting to not thank the folks who have helped so much along the way. To Khan, for an infinite supply of patience and a solid arse-kicking that put me on the right track, my eternal thanks for everything. Mike Mac, for teaching me to become not only a better chef, but also a manager. Ross Lusted, who endured many, many, many questions with patience and understanding. Catherine and Lorraine, for sharing their unfathomable knowledge. Baci, Christian and Sascha, for putting up with late menu changes, over-seasoned fish, and many other issues on a daily basis (I'll pay for them in the next life, I'm sure). Brendo, Jason and Shaun are the rocks no mountain can be without. To the other unbalanced lunatics who have come and gone, you have made Spice an awesome place to work, so thanks again. To Neil, Trish and David, my heartfelt thanks and appreciation for the monumental job you guys do. To be sitting here writing this, I feel exceedingly fortunate, and I will never forget it. Lastly, to my beautiful wife and two bozos, for all the times I have stayed back to fix dishwashers, unblock drains and everything else, I love you loads. Cheers and thanks, Andy.

Ben Pollard

Head Chef, Spice Temple Melbourne

My journey with Neil Perry began in the year 2000, when I joined his team at Rockpool Sydney as a second-year apprentice chef. Coming from Byron Bay, I'd had limited exposure to Chinese cooking, so Rockpool was a real eye-opener. The food was classified as 'modern Australian', but it was the Chinese flavours that really stood out. I was both inspired and excited.

Three years later, I moved to Melbourne to help open Rockpool Bar & Grill. A wonderful experience, this was also an invaluable stepping-stone to becoming head chef of Spice Temple, which opened just four years later.

Being invited to head up Spice Temple Melbourne made me feel like everything was falling into place. Here was the cuisine I was truly passionate about, coupled with an opportunity to explore the diversity of China's palate. So we gathered a selection of chefs, including Brendan Sheldrick (whom I am indebted to) from Spice Temple Sydney, and we found passionate suppliers like Peter Cannavo who were constantly on the lookout for different or unusual ingredients. But what really made the difference was the amount of time, energy and training Neil put into the staff. And it's paid off.

The food at Spice Temple is based around different regions of China, and this gives the menu a lot of flexibility, because the flavours and ingredients differ quite dramatically from region to region. As we are constantly on the lookout for new ideas, trips to China with Neil are of course invaluable, but inspiration also comes from cookbooks and discussions with staff.

I love seeing people's reactions to eating the food at Spice Temple. The most common is 'I have never tried anything like it!' It feels great to bring new flavours to people. Similarly, in the kitchen, I love watching new chefs as they taste everything, and seeing the amazement on their faces. For young chefs, especially, it offers not only an amazing opportunity to learn about regional Chinese cuisine, but also to work with the best produce in Australia. Without doubt, it is the quality of the produce that really sets us apart and makes us unique.

I am very proud to be a part of Spice Temple and the Rockpool Group. It has shaped my career and brought me to where I am now. Neil Perry is an amazing man and a wonderful mentor. It is with great affection that we have nicknamed him 'our fearless leader'.

Sascha Richardson

Restaurant Manager, Spice Temple Sydney

I like to think of Spice Temple Sydney as the cheeky little sister, the feminine, sexy and mysterious one in the Rockpool Group family. Though born of the same ideology, spirit and passion, she is planets apart from her Rockpool Bar & Grill brothers, and is always pushing the boundaries. Located in the sub-basement of an Art Deco building, with an unusually lit door the only sign that she exists, her discreet appearance only adds to the intrigue.

The dark and magical, opium den–like design created by Neil Perry and Grant Cheyne has proven a beautiful success, with Anton Monsted's playlists setting the mood. I liken each service to a show, each and every one different due to our diverse clientele, but the common ingredients are always exquisite food accompanied by warm and humble service.

I had spent three years working at Rockpool Bar & Grill Sydney when my manager, Jeremy Courmadias, called me into an impromptu and life-changing meeting. He told me that the awesome restaurant manager Baci Moore was about to leave Spice Temple, and asked if I would like to take over the reins. I must say this had never even been on my radar; I loved Rockpool Bar & Grill with all my heart. But of course the answer would be yes, as Neil, Trish, David and Jeremy all believed in me, as I believed in them.

Off I went to the basement. From silver service to chopsticks, plastic spoons and tofu . . . lots of it! Transported to a dark and powerful environment, I felt unsure and quite overwhelmed, and did not truly settle until our legendary head chef Andy Evans took me under his wing. His passion, knowledge and enthusiasm for Neil's vision are phenomenal, and his dedication a source of inspiration. It was Andy who would teach me about the balance of sweet, sour, salt and bitter flavours; and that it is not a health hazard to use a master stock that is six years old. It is a daily pleasure to take new guests on a journey through the Yin and Yang of the menu, always attempting to achieve balance, excitement and overall happiness.

The familiar faces of many regulars from Rockpool Bar & Grill also helped me to settle into my new role. Interestingly, at Spice Temple, they seem to want to let their hair down somewhat more. Perhaps it's something to do with the loss of a sense of time and place once you enter Spice Temple. For all we know, it could be midday or the middle of the night outside; once everyone is swept up in the all-consuming atmosphere, it really doesn't matter. People come to Spice Temple to disappear. Discreet rendezvous take place; birthdays, anniversaries and special occasions are celebrated.

I cherish and respect everything about Spice Temple, especially the amazing teams both front and back of house. We are all nurtured and guided by our brilliant leaders Neil, Trish, Andy and Jeremy. Thank you for this wonderful experience in life!

A SPICE TEMPLE
MEAL

When putting together a shared meal for family and friends, always remember the reason they are coming over is to see you. Don't attempt to cook too many stir-fries or other dishes that need a lot of last-minute preparation, otherwise you will spend all your time in the kitchen and none with your guests. Plan to cook dishes you are confident about making, and never try something for the first time on a big night. Experiment on the family – that's what they are for!

For four to six people, one dish per person is generally enough with rice, but at the most I'd suggest one dish per person, plus one dish for the table. I reckon the most you want to prepare is six dishes, so if the numbers increase, don't try to cook eight or ten dishes, just make more of each dish instead.

If you're new to Chinese cooking, start with a couple of dishes, perhaps some dumplings or a salad and a hot entrée, followed by another couple of dishes with rice. Or just do four or five dishes that you feel go well together. Generally speaking, I like to serve a stir-fry, something steamed, a braise, something deep-fried, a salad – and rice, of course. Perfect. Then, if I want more, I'd probably add another braised or steamed dish, or a couple of stir-fries if the meal is split into several courses – get someone to help, then they can serve some dishes while you make two quick stir-fries.

The other thing to think about is balance. You don't want too many chicken dishes, or beef in everything, and you should aim for some saucy and some drier dishes. Remember to use a range of cooking techniques to help you get your timing right, so you can get the meal out of the kitchen! Following are a few menu ideas for four to six people, listing dishes that go well together – feel free to swap dishes in or out, or just head straight to the recipes and start cooking up a storm if you're feeling confident.

Food and wine matching

by Sebastian Crowther, Master Sommelier

Food and wine matching can be a head-scratching affair, and I think it's fair to say that the old rules of white wine with white-fleshed fish or meat, and red wine with red meat have well and truly been tossed out the window. One key thing that is often overlooked is that if you don't like a particular wine, then it's never going to work for you with anything you're eating. That said, there are a few basic rules that will help you on your way and perhaps change your mindset.

Spice Temple is a modern Chinese restaurant that avoids the standard Cantonese fare. Rather it angles more at spice. I find the best harmony between food and wine is when I look at the spikes in the dishes. By spikes, I mean anything that stands out. So leave the main protein behind for a minute and think: What is it being served with? Is there an abundance of spice, acid, salty sauce or sweet-and-sour components?

Some shared-table menu ideas

Always have some pickles on the table – they're particularly delicious with hot fiery food, as their tartness seems to cool the palate and their crunch provides a wonderful textural contrast. And don't forget the rice. I prefer steamed rice with shared meals like these, keeping fried rice for a simple one-bowl lunch or perhaps with one other dish for a light dinner. (Any leftover steamed rice can be frozen – it makes the best fried rice.) Traditionally, dessert doesn't play a big part in an authentic Chinese meal, but if you want to finish with something sweet we've reinterpreted some Chinese flavour profiles and combined them with our knowledge of pastry to create some unique desserts (see pages 251–269).

Spinach and sesame salad 72
Deep-fried squid with heaven-facing chillies and cabbage salad 103
Jiangxi-style steamed flathead 153
Three-shot chicken: beer, chilli and soy 170
Steamed Chinese broccoli with oyster sauce 226

———

Tingling prawns 76
Lamb and cumin pancakes 113
Hot, sweet, sour and numbing pork 197
Steamed king abalone mushrooms with garlic stems, chives and ginger 240

———

Steamed eggplant with three flavours: garlic, coriander and sweet pork 75
Hot and numbing dried beef 109
Lucky duck noodles with pickled vegetables 130
Stir-fried prawns with salted duck egg and four chillies 162
Guangxi-style crisp pork belly with coriander, peanuts, red onion and sesame seeds 194
Greens stir-fried with garlic 222

———

Prawn wontons with black vinegar and chilli 32
Tea-smoked duck breast with pickled cabbage and mustard dressing 80
Hunan-style steamed blue-eye trevalla with salted red chillies and pickled green chilli 154
Stir-fried quail and peanuts with steamed egg custard 174
Snake beans stir-fried with pork and XO sauce 244

———

Bang-bang chicken 79
Salt and pepper silken tofu with spicy coriander salad 98
Stir-fried spanner crab with leek, salted chilli and yellow beans 165
Stir-fried cumin lamb 208
Peas stir-fried with soy beans, mustard greens and pork belly 243

Spicy or chilli-laden dishes can play havoc with acidic wine. Acidic whites will become very hard and overly heavy or tannic; reds with high alcohol or oak will feel like you're throwing fuel on the fire, becoming very astringent and unpleasant. In this instance, look for fruity whites, or those that have a little sweetness. If you're a red-drinker, then look for a light- to medium-bodied red that is soft and silky. Less-complex, reasonably priced wines will handle these situations best.

Another element that might cause an issue is sweetness. Here the problem is finding a wine to balance. If the wine is not sweet enough, then it will seem overly acidic and dry. If it is too sweet, it will override the flavours of the dish.

Salty dishes can play a similar trick on wines. Avoid structured reds. Rosés and whites are your best bet. With regards to sour dishes where citrus stands tall, I like to match acid with acid. Look to dry, crisp whites for harmony.

Finally, think about balance. Try to match the intensity of the wine with that of the dish. Above all else, you should drink what you like – but do not be afraid to explore new things. Experiment and have fun. Spice Temple's wine team and wait staff are always on hand to help you find a hidden treasure or point you in the right direction. If that doesn't entice, there are always juices, beers and cocktails. Over to you, Mr Healy.

Juices, beers and cocktails

by Richard Healy

We shouldn't forget how wonderfully the food at Spice Temple works with others drinks, such as juices, beers and our ever-evolving list of cocktails. Inspired by the 12 zodiac signs of the Chinese calendar, our cocktails also change seasonally.

More and more, we are finding that diners love to experiment with drinking cocktails alongside their meals. We tend to find that citrus-dominant drinks work well with the hotter, more spicy dishes. Simple, classic cocktails, such as an Army & Navy (gin, lemon juice and orgeat) or similar drinks, will help to placate the spice without dumbing down any of the nuances of the dish. Broader, weightier and more powerful cocktails like Manhattans can be difficult to pair with this kind of food, due to the intensity and profile of the flavours. Perhaps these are best left for enjoying pre- or post-dining.

Beer is also popular, and makes a smart pairing. Styles of beer that work well with many of the dishes include pale ales and pilsners. While being lighter in body, pilsners will often display notes of citrus and gentle spice, a profile that marries perfectly with the food at Spice Temple. If you want to be more adventurous, try Gueuze, a style of Lambic beer. Leaning towards the bitter or sour side, and with higher acidity, it heightens many of the flavours, including the perceived level of spice – and the way it cuts through the richer dishes is a revelation.

BASIC
PREPARATIONS

CHILLI SAUCE

Makes about 250 ml (1 cup)

Serve this as a dipping sauce for dumplings or as a condiment. Stored in a sterilised jar, it will keep indefinitely in the fridge.

500 g fresh long red chillies, seeds removed,
　　roughly chopped
3 cloves garlic, peeled
300 ml canola oil
2 teaspoons sea salt
1 tablespoon white sugar
2½ tablespoons light soy sauce

Pound the chillies and garlic using a mortar and pestle, or process in a blender, until you have a rough paste. Gradually add the oil, blending to a smooth consistency.

Transfer the chilli purée to a heavy-based saucepan. Add the salt and sugar and cook over low heat, stirring occasionally, for 45 minutes or until the sauce turns bright red and the rawness has been cooked out. Remove from the heat and stir in the soy sauce. Taste and adjust the seasoning.

SWEET CHILLI SAUCE

Makes about 500 ml (2 cups)

Serve this as a dipping sauce for deep-fried food or dumplings. Stored in a sterilised jar or bottle, it will keep indefinitely in the fridge.

500 ml (2 cups) vegetable oil
3 cloves garlic, finely sliced
20 g ginger, cut into fine julienne strips
500 g caster sugar
500 ml (2 cups) rice wine vinegar
3 fresh long red chillies, seeds removed, cut into fine
　　julienne strips

In a wok, heat the oil to 180°C. Add the garlic and deep-fry, stirring constantly, until it turns light golden brown. Using a slotted spoon, quickly remove the garlic and drain on paper towel, then spread it out to dry and become crisp. Repeat the process for the ginger.

Combine the sugar, vinegar and chilli in a heavy-based saucepan. Place over medium heat and bring to the boil, stirring until the sugar has dissolved, then turn the heat down to low and simmer until the sauce has reduced by almost half. Remove the pan from the heat and, using your fingers, crumble the deep-fried garlic and ginger into the sauce, then stir through.

FRESH CHILLI SAUCE

Makes about 100 ml

Make this sauce fresh every time you wish to serve it, then offer in small sauce dishes at a banquet or with dumplings.

4 fresh long red chillies
4 cloves garlic, peeled
1 tablespoon rice wine vinegar
2 teaspoons white sugar
½ teaspoon sea salt

Pound the chillies and garlic using a mortar and pestle until you have a paste. Stir in the rest of the ingredients, then taste and adjust the seasoning if necessary.

XO SAUCE

Makes about 250 ml (1 cup)

With many variations, this is our go-to sauce at Spice Temple, made from chilli, dried scallop and dried shrimp, cooked very slowly in oil until rich and fragrant. We serve it with dumplings or steamed rice, as well as using it in fried rice, noodle and vegetable dishes. Stored in a sterilised jar, it will keep indefinitely in the fridge.

4 dried scallops (conpoy)
50 g dried shrimp
warm water, for soaking
200 g fresh long red chillies, seeds removed, finely chopped
50 g ginger, finely chopped
50 g garlic, finely chopped
30 g sea salt
30 g white sugar
300 ml vegetable oil
3 spring onions, finely sliced

In separate bowls, soak the dried scallops and shrimp in warm water for 2 hours, then drain.

Place the scallops on a heatproof plate. Place in a bamboo steamer, cover with the lid and steam over a saucepan or wok of rapidly boiling water for 10 minutes. Remove the scallops from the steamer and, while they are still warm, shred them with your fingers, separating all the fibres.

Pound the shrimp using a mortar and pestle or grind in an electric spice grinder until finely ground.

Place all the ingredients, except the spring onion, in a large, heavy-based saucepan and cook over low heat, stirring occasionally, for 45 minutes or until the sauce loses its raw taste and turns a deep red colour. Remove from the heat and leave to cool, then stir through the spring onions.

DARK CHILLI PASTE

Makes about 750 g (1 cup)

Serve this with dumplings or as a condiment. Stored in a sterilised jar, it will keep indefinitely.

500 g fresh long red chillies
120 g red onion, roughly chopped
75 g ginger, roughly chopped
50 g garlic, roughly chopped
30 g sea salt
300 ml vegetable oil

Place all the ingredients in a blender or food processor and blend to a rough paste. Transfer to a large heavy-based saucepan and cook over very low heat for 4 hours or until the chilli paste is dark and richly flavoured.

FERMENTED RED CHILLIES

Makes about 1 kg

The complex, nuanced taste of these fermented chillies adds an extra dimension of flavour to stir-fries, such as stir-fried prawns with salted duck egg and four chillies (see page 162) or stir-fried cumin lamb (see page 208). In six years of making these at Spice Temple, we've never had any problems with black mould – but if any does develop as the chillies ferment, they may be dangerous to eat and must be discarded.

1 kg fresh long red chillies, rinsed, dried and cut into
   1 cm lengths
50 ml water
50 g white sugar
30 g sea salt
5 star anise
5 cassia bark sticks

Place the chillies in a large, heatproof bowl. In a small saucepan, bring the water, sugar and salt to the boil. Remove from the heat and add the star anise and cassia bark, then pour over the chillies. Toss to coat well. Spread the chillies over a clean plastic tray and wrap tightly with cling film, then punch small holes in the film to allow air in and out. Leave the tray on the bench overnight.

Next day, unwrap the chillies and stir to coat again, then re-wrap with fresh cling film, again piercing holes in the surface. Repeat this process every day for 3 weeks. During this time, a thin fluffy white mould will develop on the chillies – it is this natural mould that changes their flavour. Remember to stir the chillies every day, and to keep all trays and utensils scrupulously clean. If any black mould appears, this indicates the presence of harmful bacteria, and you must discard that batch entirely and start again.

Once the chillies are deep red and dry, like a sun-dried tomato, they can be kept indefinitely in a sterilised glass jar at room temperature.

SICHUAN SAUCE

Makes about 200 ml

This is one of my all-time favourite sauces.

1½ tablespoons light soy sauce
45 ml Chinkiang black vinegar
2 tablespoons caster sugar
60 ml (¼ cup) chilli oil
1 teaspoon finely grated ginger
1 teaspoon finely grated garlic
2 tablespoons dried chilli flakes
1 tablespoon finely chopped spring onion
2 teaspoons roasted and ground Sichuan
   pepper (see page 17)
2 teaspoons Laoganma chilli crisp sauce
1 tablespoon finely chopped coriander
1½ tablespoons Chinese chicken stock (see page 17) or water

Place all the ingredients in a small bowl and mix together well.

SALTED CHILLIES

Makes about 1 kg

Used as an ingredient in fish and meat dishes, these chillies will easily keep for a few months.

1 kg fresh long red chillies
150 g sea salt

Rinse and dry the chillies. Trim off the stems and roughly chop the chillies, then mix with three-quarters of the sea salt in a bowl. Pack the chilli and salt mixture into a sterilised glass jar, sprinkle with the rest of the sea salt and seal with the lid.

Store the jar in a cool, dark place for at least 2 weeks before using. Refrigerate after opening.

PICKLED GREEN CHILLIES

Makes about 200 g

Stored in a sterilised jar, these chillies will keep indefinitely in the fridge. Use them in vegetable dishes, such as fish fragrant eggplant (see page 100).

100 ml white vinegar
100 g caster sugar
200 g fresh long green chillies, cut crossways into 1 cm slices

Place the vinegar and sugar in a small stainless-steel saucepan and bring to the boil, stirring to dissolve the sugar. When the sugar has dissolved, remove from the heat and leave to cool.

Meanwhile, pack the chilli slices into a sterilised glass jar. When the pickling liquid is cool, pour it over the chillies, then seal the jar and refrigerate. Leave for a month before using.

PICKLED CUCUMBER

Makes about 2 cups

200 ml rice wine vinegar
200 g caster sugar
2 small (Lebanese) cucumbers, sliced

Bring the vinegar to a simmer in a small heavy-based saucepan, add the sugar and stir until dissolved. Remove from the heat and leave to cool.

Place the cucumber in the cooled pickling liquid in a sterilised jar and leave at room temperature to pickle for 3 hours, then store in the fridge for up to 2 weeks.

ROASTED AND GROUND SICHUAN PEPPER

Makes about 1 teaspoon

Once ground, the flavour and fragrance of Sichuan pepper starts to diminish, so it's best to make it in small quantities that will get used up quite quickly.

1 tablespoon Sichuan peppercorns

Briefly roast the peppercorns over medium heat in a small heavy-based frying pan until fragrant, then grind in a spice or coffee grinder or crush using a mortar and pestle.

SICHUAN PEPPER AND SALT

Makes about 125 g

This condiment lasts well for several months in an airtight container away from direct sunlight. Its flavour and aroma dissipates over time, though, so don't keep it for too long.

100 g sea salt
35 g Sichuan peppercorns

Preheat the oven to 180°C. Place the sea salt and peppercorns on a baking tray and roast for 5–6 minutes or until fragrant. Leave to cool, then grind to a very fine powder in a spice grinder or using a mortar and pestle. Pass through a fine sieve, discarding any debris left in the sieve.

SPRING ONION OIL

Makes about 150 ml

Stored in a sterilised bottle or jar, spring onion oil will keep in the fridge for up to 2 weeks. Use this vibrant green oil to dress salads and noodles. Never cook it, or its fresh flavour and bright colour will be destroyed.

200 ml vegetable oil
small handful of spring onion tops, roughly chopped

Combine the oil and spring onion tops in a small heavy-based saucepan, place over low heat and warm until the oil reaches 80°C.

Remove the infused oil from the heat and leave to cool slightly. Transfer to a blender and blend until smooth, then strain through a muslin-lined sieve.

CHINESE CHICKEN STOCK

Makes about 2 litres

If you don't want to waste the chicken after it has given its flavour to the stock, you can use the meat in fried rice or noodle dishes, but remember it will be quite dry. The stock can be stored for three days in the fridge, or around three months in the freezer.

1 × 1.6 kg free-range or organic chicken
2 slices ginger
1 spring onion, cut into 4 cm lengths
3 litres cold water

Remove any excess fat from the cavity of the chicken, then rinse under cold water and pat dry with paper towel. Chop the chicken Chinese-style (see page 18), then place in a stockpot or heavy-based saucepan large enough to fit the chicken snugly and add the rest of the ingredients. Bring to the boil, then reduce the heat to a low simmer. Thoroughly skim off the froth from the surface of the stock, then simmer for 30 minutes, skimming continually.

Further reduce the heat until the surface is barely moving and cook for 2 hours. Remove the stock from the heat and strain through a muslin-lined sieve. For a crystal-clear stock, strain again before using or storing.

MASTER STOCK

Makes about 3 litres

This rich stock is used to braise meats, infusing them with flavour and colour as they cook. After each use, strain your master stock into a clean pan and bring it back to the boil. Pour the stock into an airtight container, cool and then freeze. Next time you want to use your master stock, just place the stock in a pot, top it up with some water and more of the aromatics and seasoning ingredients (about three-quarters of the amounts listed below) and bring back to a simmer . . . and you're well on your way to becoming a master stocker.

2.5 litres cold water
500 ml (2 cups) light soy sauce
250 ml (1 cup) Shaoxing wine
125 g yellow rock sugar, crushed
handful of spring onion tops
10 cm knob of ginger, sliced
8 cloves garlic, sliced
4 star anise
2 cinnamon sticks
3 pieces dried tangerine peel

Place all the ingredients in a stockpot or large heavy-based saucepan. Bring to the boil, then reduce the heat to low and simmer for 30 minutes. (If not using straightaway, pour the stock into an airtight container, cool slightly, then freeze.)

MASTER-STOCK CHICKEN

Serves 4–6 as part of a shared meal

1 × 1.6 kg free-range or organic chicken
3 litres master stock (see above)
1 spring onion, white part only, cut into fine julienne strips
freshly ground white pepper

Remove any excess fat from the cavity of the chicken and wipe it clean. Bring a stockpot or large heavy-based saucepan of water to the boil, plunge the chicken into it and leave for 1 minute, then remove and rinse under cold running water. Pat the chicken dry with paper towel.

Rinse out the pan, then add the master stock. Bring to the boil, then reduce the heat and simmer for 30 minutes. Submerge the chicken in the stock, and increase the heat to return to the boil. Adjust the heat to a high simmer and cook the chicken, uncovered, for 20 minutes. Turn the chicken over and simmer for a further 3 minutes, then place a lid on the pan, remove from the heat and leave the chicken to cool in the stock. Once the stock has completely cooled, remove the chicken and drain the stock from the cavity.

Chop the chicken (see left) and arrange on a serving plate. Strain the master stock through a fine sieve and discard the aromatics, then pour 250 ml (1 cup) of the stock into a small pan and simmer until reduced by half. Pour this reduced stock over the chicken, scatter over the spring onion and a good grinding of white pepper, then serve.

WHITE-CUT CHICKEN

Serves 4–6 as part of a shared meal

This is a classic Chinese way of preparing chicken, resulting in very moist and tender meat that can be used in salads, and rice and noodles dishes or simply served with ginger and spring onion dressing (see page 179).

1 × 1.6–1.8 kg free-range or organic chicken
250 ml (1 cup) Shaoxing wine
6 spring onions, dark green parts only
3 cloves garlic, sliced
5 cm knob of ginger, sliced
3.5 litres water
ice

Remove any excess fat from the cavity of the chicken, then rinse under cold water and pat dry with paper towel. Take a stockpot or heavy-based saucepan large enough to hold the chicken snugly. Place the Shaoxing wine, spring onions, garlic, ginger and water into the pan. Bring to the boil, then immerse the chicken in the stock and return to the boil. Let it bubble away for 5 minutes, skimming away any froth that rises to the surface, then reduce the heat to a high simmer. Place a tight-fitting lid on the pan and simmer for 15 minutes. Remove from the heat and leave the chicken to steep for 20 minutes (do not be tempted to lift the lid or the heat will dissipate).

Remove the lid and carefully lift the chicken from the stock. Drain the liquid from the cavity and submerge the chicken in a large bowl or sink of iced water, leaving it to cool for 15 minutes. Thoroughly drain the chicken, place it on a plate and chill in the fridge for at least 4 hours to completely set the juices.

Chop the chicken (see below), arrange on a platter and serve with your choice of dressing.

CHOPPING CHICKEN OR DUCK

To chop a raw or cooked chicken or duck in the Chinese style, place the bird on a chopping board with its legs facing away from you. Cut the bird in half lengthways with a cleaver. Lay one half in front of you and cut off the leg, then cut off the wing where it joins at the breast. Cut the wing lengthways, then cut the leg into 6 pieces. Slice the breast into 6 pieces. Repeat with the other half.

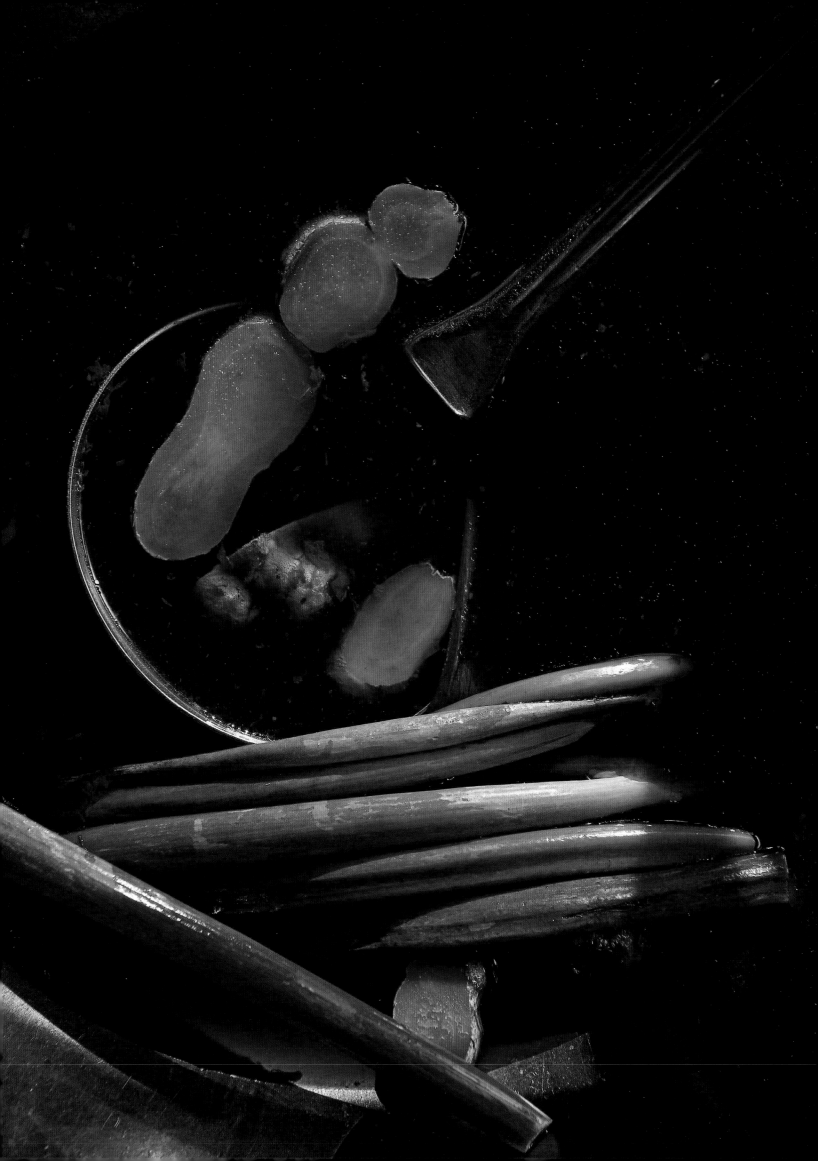

RED-BRAISED DUCK

Serves 4–6 as part of a shared meal

At the restaurant, we debone the braised duck and then press it in the fridge overnight, but at home you can just shred the meat from the carcass before using it in Aromatic duck salad with tea eggs and coriander (see page 70), Lucky duck noodles with pickled vegetables (see page 130) and Ma po of shredded duck, silken tofu, chestnuts and pickled vegetables (see page 186). Red-braised duck will keep for several days in the fridge.

3 litres master stock (see page 18)
1 × 2 kg duck, neck, wings and parson's nose removed

Place the stock in a large heavy-based saucepan and bring to the boil. Gently lower the duck into the stock, then turn off the heat and leave the liquid to cool. Make sure the duck is completely submerged in the stock – you may need to weight it down with a small plate – before transferring to the fridge and leaving for 24 hours.

The next day, lift the duck out of the stock, place in a steamer basket and steam for 80 minutes over rapidly boiling water, topping up the water as needed. Remove and, when the duck is cool enough to handle, cut it in half and shred the duck meat from the carcass.

RED-BRAISED LAMB SHOULDER

Serves 4–6 as part of a shared meal

Deeply flavoured, this shredded lamb can be stored in a covered container in the fridge for up to a week. Serve in Gua bao (see page 62) or with salted chillies (see page 15).

3 litres master stock (see page 18)
1 kg lamb shoulder on the bone, trimmed of excess fat

Place the stock in a stockpot or large heavy-based saucepan and bring to the boil. Add the lamb, then reduce the heat to a simmer and braise the lamb very slowly for 2 hours or until soft and falling apart.

Remove from the heat and leave to cool to room temperature, then transfer the pan of lamb and stock to the refrigerator. When the stock is cold, remove the layer of solidified fat from the surface and discard, then take the lamb out of the stock and shred the meat.

RED-BRAISED BRISKET

Makes about 750 g

Braising the brisket in the oven helps to keep the temperature low and steady, but you could also slowly braise the meat on the stovetop over a very low heat. The cooked brisket can be kept in the fridge for up to a week, ready for use in Hot and numbing dried beef (see page 109), or to go with yellow noodles (see page 122) or lucky money dumplings (see page 216).

3 litres master stock (see page 18)
1 kg beef brisket

Preheat the oven to 170°C.

Place the stock in an ovenproof saucepan or flameproof casserole and bring to the boil. Taste for seasoning and adjust accordingly. Lower the brisket into the stock, then cover and transfer to the oven. Braise the brisket for 3 hours or until tender and falling apart, checking the liquid level every so often and topping up with water as needed to make sure the meat is covered with the stock.

PRESSED PORK BELLY

Makes about 300 g

This rich pork can be stored in a covered container in the fridge for up to a week. Slice and use in braises or stir-fries, such as Peas stir-fried with soy beans and mustard greens (see page 243).

1 × 400 g piece boneless pork belly, about 10 cm wide
100 g ginger, sliced
2 litres water
60 g fine salt

Place all the ingredients in a heavy-based saucepan and bring to a simmer, then turn off the heat and leave the pork to cool in the liquid. Remove the pork and place on a plate or tray lined with baking paper, place another piece of baking paper over the pork and another plate or tray on top of that. Weight with tins of food or similar to press the meat, then refrigerate overnight.

CRISPY PORK BELLY

Makes about 750 g

Serve this Guangxi-style with coriander, peanuts, red onion and sesame seeds (see page 194), in sliders (see page 67), or with fried rice and noodles. If you have any left over, it can be kept in the fridge for three days.

1 kg pork belly
sea salt

Place the pork belly on a wire rack set over a plate (to catch any drips) and refrigerate, uncovered, for 2 days to dry the skin out.

Preheat the oven to 190°C. Transfer the pork belly to a roasting tin, then, using a sharp knife, score the skin deeply in a diamond pattern and rub generously with sea salt. Roast the pork for 20 minutes, then reduce the temperature to 170°C and roast for a further 20 minutes or until the meat is cooked through and the skin is blistered and crispy.

Remove the pork from the oven, cover with foil and set aside in a warm place to rest for 20 minutes before using.

TEA-SMOKING MIXTURE

Makes 300 g

This mixture can be made well in advance and kept in an airtight container for use at a later date – it will keep well for several months.

100 g jasmine tea leaves
100 g soft brown sugar
100 g (½ cup) jasmine rice

Simply combine all the ingredients and use as instructed in the recipe.

TEA EGGS

Makes 6

Serve these beautiful, crackle-glazed eggs with Cucumbers with smashed garlic and ginger (see page 27), pickled cabbage and radish (see page 24), some BBQ pork (see page 192) or White-cut chicken (see page 18) and Chilli sauce (see page 14). You will need to prepare these at least 24 hours before serving.

6 free-range or organic eggs
2 tablespoons jasmine tea leaves
3 cassia bark sticks
3 star anise
1 teaspoon sea salt
60 ml (¼ cup) dark soy sauce

Place the eggs in a small saucepan, cover with water and bring to the boil. Simmer for 10 minutes, then drain and plunge into a sink or bowl of cold water. Gently tap the eggs with the back of a spoon until the shell is covered with small cracks, then return the eggs to the pan and cover with fresh water. Add the rest of the ingredients, then simmer gently for 1 hour. Remove from the heat and leave to cool slightly before transferring to the fridge. Leave the eggs to infuse for at least 24 hours before using.

To serve, take the eggs out of the stock, remove the shells and place in a serving bowl.

DEEP-FRIED SHALLOTS

Makes about 60 g

Used as a garnish for salads, noodle dishes and whole fish, these keep well in an airtight container in a cool dark place.

100 ml vegetable oil
100 g red shallots, finely sliced using a mandoline
sea salt

Heat a wok until smoking, pour in the oil and heat to 160°C. Add the shallot and deep-fry, stirring often, until golden.

Remove the deep-fried shallots with a slotted spoon and drain well on paper towel. Season lightly with sea salt.

PICKLES

CABBAGE AND RADISH

Makes about 1.75 kg

This pickle will get better the longer you leave it. Unopened jars can be stored
for several months in a cool dark place, or indefinitely in the refrigerator.
Serve it with a little dark chilli paste on top for a bit of extra spice and salt.

CABBAGE AND RADISH

800 g savoy cabbage, cut into 2 cm chunks
800 g red radishes, cut in half
100 g sea salt

In a large glass or ceramic bowl, toss the cabbage and radish with the salt and leave
for 1 hour.

PICKLING LIQUID

400 ml rice wine vinegar
400 g white sugar

Pour the vinegar into a large heavy-based saucepan and bring to the boil, then add
the sugar and stir until it dissolves. Remove this pickling liquid from the heat and
leave to cool to room temperature.

Rinse the salted cabbage and radish, then drain thoroughly. Firmly pack the
cabbage and radish into glass jars. Gradually pour the pickling liquid into the jars,
waiting for it to find its way to the bottom of each jar before adding more. Seal
with a tight-fitting lid and leave in a cool dark place for at least 2 days before using.

CUCUMBERS WITH SMASHED GARLIC AND GINGER

Makes about 350 g

These will keep in the fridge for a few days. Bring back to room temperature before serving.

4 small (Lebanese) cucumbers, cut into quarters lengthways and seeds removed

40 g sea salt

PREPARING THE CUCUMBERS

Cut the cucumber into thin strips about 5 cm long. Place in a colander set over a bowl, sprinkle with the sea salt and mix to coat well. Leave to stand for 1 hour to draw out the excess moisture, then rinse under cold running water and drain thoroughly.

1 large knob of ginger, peeled and cut into very fine julienne strips

30 g caster sugar

2 tablespoons rice wine vinegar

2 teaspoons sesame oil

10 cloves garlic, finely chopped

PICKLING MIXTURE

Transfer the cucumber to a bowl, add the rest of the ingredients and stir well for 1 minute, then leave to marinate for 5 minutes before serving.

PEANUTS IN AGED BLACK VINEGAR

Makes about 100 g

This pickle tastes especially good when the liquid is really cold. The pickling
liquid will keep well for several months in the fridge in an airtight container,
ready for when you next want to serve this as an appetiser.

PICKLING LIQUID

225 ml Chinkiang black vinegar
150 ml light soy sauce
25 g caster sugar
500 ml (2 cups) water

Put the vinegar, soy sauce, sugar and water into a non-reactive saucepan. Stir over medium heat for 5 minutes or until all the sugar has dissolved. Remove from the heat and leave to cool at room temperature, then chill in the fridge until nice and cold.

TO SERVE

100 g small roasted unsalted peanuts, skin on
¼ small (Lebanese) cucumber, finely diced
a few coriander leaves

Place the roasted peanuts in a small bowl and pour enough of the cold pickling liquid over until it just covers the peanuts. Garnish with the cucumber and coriander.

DUMPLINGS AND THINGS

PRAWN WONTONS WITH
BLACK VINEGAR AND CHILLI

Makes about 80

These were among the first dumplings we made at Spice Temple. The slippery
texture of boiled wonton skins with the firm prawn filling is made even more
addictive by the sour and hot sauce. If you're not up for making the wonton
skin dough from scratch, just use ready-made wonton skins to make these.
We make this in large batches for the restaurant, but you could always freeze
half before cooking.

WONTON SKIN DOUGH

300 g (2 cups) plain flour,
plus extra for dusting
1 egg yolk
150 ml water
1 teaspoon sea salt
1 teaspoon vegetable oil

Sift the flour into a bowl and make a well in the centre. Add the rest of the
ingredients to the well, then use a wooden spoon to bring the dough together.
Tip out the dough onto a floured bench and, using your hands, knead for 5 minutes
or until smooth and elastic. Wrap in cling film and set aside to rest for 30 minutes.

PRAWN FILLING

20 g shredded Chinese cabbage (wombok)
1 teaspoon sea salt
200 g raw prawn meat, roughly chopped
2 teaspoons Shaoxing wine
1 teaspoon sesame oil

Place the cabbage in a colander with a bowl underneath and sprinkle over the salt.
Leave for 20 minutes to draw out the excess moisture, then rinse well and use your
hands to squeeze dry. Place in a bowl and mix in the rest of the ingredients. Cover
and refrigerate while you make the dressing and roll the dough.

BLACK VINEGAR AND CHILLI DRESSING

1½ tablespoons Chinkiang black vinegar
25 ml light soy sauce
1 tablespoon caster sugar
60 ml (¼ cup) chilli oil
1 tablespoon finely grated ginger
2 teaspoons finely grated garlic
2 teaspoons dried chilli flakes
1 spring onion, finely sliced
2 teaspoons roasted and ground
Sichuan pepper (see page 17)

Combine all the ingredients in a small bowl.

TO FILL AND SHAPE THE WONTONS

Roll the dough through a pasta machine until it is 1.5 mm thick. Place strips of
the dough on a floured bench and cut into 10 cm squares. Place 1 teaspoon
of the filling in the centre of each wonton skin. Brush the edges of the wonton
skin with water and fold into a triangle shape, pressing to seal the edges. Repeat
until all the filling is used. (Any leftover wonton skins can be wrapped in cling film
and kept in the fridge for 2–3 days or frozen for up to 3 months.)

TO FINISH

Cook the wontons in a saucepan of rapidly boiling water for 2 minutes. Remove
from the water with a slotted spoon or Chinese strainer, drain and place in bowls.
Spoon over some of the dressing and serve.

NORTHERN-STYLE LAMB AND FENNEL DUMPLINGS

Makes about 80

I first ate these little beauties at the restaurant inside the Xinjiang provincial government offices in Beijing, and promptly fell in love with them. Similar to a pot sticker, with a crisp base and chewy top, they have a rich, aniseed-flavoured filling. Serve with dark chilli paste (see page 15). We make these in large batches at Spice Temple, but you could always freeze half before cooking.

150 g (1 cup) plain flour, plus extra for dusting
350 g potato starch
450 ml boiling water

DUMPLING DOUGH

Sift the flour and potato starch into a bowl. Pour in the boiling water and mix with a wooden spoon until a dough forms, then tip out onto a floured bench and knead for 5 minutes or until smooth. Cover with a bowl and leave to rest for 10 minutes.

500 g fatty lamb mince
1 tablespoon fennel seeds, toasted and ground
7 cm knob of ginger, finely chopped
2 spring onions, finely sliced
¾ teaspoon sea salt
¾ teaspoon white sugar
25 ml light soy sauce
25 ml sesame oil
20 g potato starch

LAMB FILLING

Mix all the ingredients together in a bowl.

TO FILL AND SHAPE THE DUMPLINGS

Divide the dough into walnut-sized balls and set aside, covered with a bowl. Use a small rolling pin to roll out a dough ball into a round about 10 cm in diameter. Place a tablespoon of the lamb filling in the middle and fold in half to make a half-moon shape. Pleat the top of the dumpling into a series of folds to seal, then dip the bottom into some extra flour to prevent it sticking to the frying pan. Repeat with the rest of the dough balls and filling.

TO COOK THE DUMPLINGS

vegetable oil, for pan-frying
about 500 ml (2 cups) Chinese chicken stock (see page 17) or water, or as needed

Pour a film of oil into a large heavy-based frying pan over medium–high heat. Working in batches, add the dumplings in a single layer, with their pleated side facing up. When they start to sizzle, pour enough chicken stock into the pan to come about a quarter of the way up the sides of the dumplings.

Cover with a lid and reduce the heat to medium. When all the stock has evaporated, the dumplings will sizzle and pop. Remove the lid and cook for a few more minutes or until a crust forms on the bottoms of the dumplings. Carefully transfer the dumplings to serving bowls.

NORTHERN-STYLE
STEAMED PORK BUNS

Makes about 30

Made with a northern-style steamed bun dough, these dumplings are first
steamed and then fried. Serve with small bowls of soy sauce and dark chilli
paste (see page 15) to the side.

500 g skinless pork belly, cut into 3 cm chunks
40 g yellow rock sugar, crushed
50 ml Shaoxing wine
375 ml (1½ cups) Chinese chicken stock
(see page 17)
½ cinnamon stick
1 star anise
2 teaspoons finely chopped ginger
2 cloves garlic, finely chopped
90 ml light soy sauce
1 tablespoon hoisin sauce
1 tablespoon oyster sauce
25 g potato starch
100 ml water

PORK FILLING

Place all the ingredients except the potato starch and water in a heavy-based
saucepan, then bring to a simmer and simmer for 20–30 minutes or until the pork
is tender. Remove the pork from the pan using a slotted spoon and leave to cool
slightly. Keep simmering the sauce in the pan until it has reduced by half.

Make a potato starch paste by whisking the potato starch and water together
until smooth. While the sauce is reducing, gradually add some of the paste, whisking
continuously, until the sauce thickens slightly – you may not need all of the paste.
Remove and discard the cinnamon stick and star anise.

When the pork is cool enough to handle, shred it roughly with your hands or
cut into small dice, then return it to the sauce and mix well. Transfer the filling to
a bowl and leave to chill in the fridge – it needs to be cold before it is put into the
bun dough.

500 g (3⅓ cups) Hong Kong flour,
plus extra for dusting
1 teaspoon caster sugar
1 teaspoon dried yeast
300 ml tepid water

BUN DOUGH

Sift the flour and sugar into a bowl. Dissolve the yeast in the tepid water, then stir
into the dry ingredients with a wooden spoon until a dough forms. Tip out
the dough onto a floured bench and knead for 10 minutes or until smooth.
Wrap the dough in cling film and leave to rest for 10 minutes.

TO FILL AND SHAPE THE PORK BUNS

Remove the dough and punch lightly to knock it back, then knead for another
5 minutes or until smooth and elastic. Divide into golfball-sized balls, keeping
them covered with cling film to prevent the dough drying out.

On a floured bench, roll out each ball into a round about 10 cm in diameter.
Place 2 tablespoons of the filling in the middle of each round, then bring the edges
together and twist to seal at the top. Leave the buns, covered with cling film, in
a nice warm spot to prove for 15 minutes or until slightly risen.

vegetable oil, for pan-frying
500 ml (2 cups) Chinese chicken stock
(see page 17) or water, or as needed

TO COOK THE DUMPLINGS

Pour a film of oil into a large heavy-based frying pan over medium–high heat.
Working in batches, add the dumplings in a single layer, with their pleated side
facing up. When they start to sizzle, pour enough chicken stock into the pan to
come about a quarter of the way up the sides of the dumplings.

Cover with a lid and reduce the heat to medium. When all the stock has
evaporated, the dumplings will sizzle and pop. Remove the lid and cook for a few
more minutes or until a crust forms on the bottoms of the dumplings.

TO FINISH

Carefully transfer the dumplings to a serving platter and serve with soy sauce and
dark chilli paste.

CRYSTAL JADE SCALLOP AND CRAB DUMPLINGS

Makes about 20

These dumplings are named for the almost transparent, crystalline quality of the dough used to make them – a combination of wheat starch and potato starch gives just the right chewy texture. Serve these delicate dumplings with a little soy sauce or chilli sauce (see page 14).

CRYSTAL JADE DOUGH

110 g wheat starch
125 g potato starch
300 ml boiling water

Place the wheat starch and half of the potato starch in a bowl. Pour in the boiling water, stirring constantly with a wooden spoon, then leave the mixture to sit for 5 minutes. Add the rest of the potato starch and mix again with a wooden spoon until a dough forms. Tip out the dough onto a floured bench and knead for 5 minutes or until very smooth, then wrap the dough in cling film and leave to rest for 10 minutes.

SCALLOP AND CRAB FILLING

125 g raw scallop meat, cut into 3.5 cm dice
125 g raw spanner crab meat
pinch of freshly ground white pepper
1 small spring onion, finely chopped
1½ tablespoons light soy sauce
1 teaspoon finely chopped ginger
½ teaspoon sesame oil

Combine all the ingredients in a bowl.

TO FILL AND SHAPE THE DUMPLINGS

vegetable oil, for greasing

Divide the dough into walnut-sized balls, keeping them covered with cling film to prevent them drying out. Place each ball on a lightly oiled wooden chopping board and use the blade of a cleaver or large knife to squash it with a smearing motion into a rough round about 9 cm in diameter. Place a teaspoon of filling in the centre of the round and fold the dumpling in half, pressing only the outer edges to seal, then use your fingers to gently push the sides slightly inwards to create a small opening at the top. Press the bottom onto the bench to flatten the base, then place on a lightly oiled tray or plate while you fill and shape the rest of the dumplings.

TO FINISH

Steam the dumplings in batches in a lightly oiled steamer basket over simmering water for 3 minutes or until the wrappers are translucent.

HAR GOW STEAMED PRAWN DUMPLINGS

Makes about 20

For this yum cha staple, the skill lies in the pleating of the dough when shaping
each dumpling. The more pleats, and the more defined they are, the better.
Serve these classic translucent dumplings with soy sauce and chilli sauce (see page 14).

HAR GOW DOUGH

110 g wheat starch, plus extra for dusting
125 g potato starch
300 ml boiling water

Place the wheat starch and half of the potato starch in a bowl. Pour in the boiling water, stirring constantly with a wooden spoon, then leave the mixture to sit for 5 minutes. Add the rest of the potato starch and mix again with a wooden spoon until a dough forms. Tip out the dough onto a floured bench and knead for 5 minutes or until very smooth, then wrap the dough in cling film and leave to rest for 10 minutes.

PRAWN FILLING

240 g raw prawn meat
2 spring onions, finely chopped
1 tablespoon sesame oil
2 teaspoons sea salt
¼ teaspoon freshly ground white pepper

Use a sharp knife to chop the prawn meat into roughly 1 cm pieces – you really want to keep the texture of the prawns in the dumpling. Place the prawn meat in a bowl, add the rest of the ingredients and mix well.

TO FILL AND SHAPE THE DUMPLINGS

vegetable oil, for greasing

Divide the dough into walnut-sized balls, keeping them covered with cling film to prevent the dough drying out. Place each ball on a lightly oiled wooden chopping board and use the blade of a cleaver or large knife to squash it with a smearing motion into a rough round about 9 cm in diameter. Make three deep pleats in one half of each round to form a little crescent-shaped cap. Fill the dumpling with a tablespoon of the prawn mixture and press the edges together, then place on a lightly oiled tray or plate while you fill and shape the rest of the dumplings.

TO FINISH

Steam the dumplings in batches in a single layer in a lightly oiled steamer basket over simmering water for 3 minutes or until the wrappers are translucent.

PORK AND PRAWN SIU MAI

Makes about 35

These open-topped dumplings are easy to make, especially if you use bought
round wonton wrappers. Serve with soy sauce and chilli sauce (see page 14).
The dumplings can be frozen prior to cooking.

SIU MAI DOUGH

300 g (2 cups) plain flour,
plus extra for dusting
1 egg yolk
150 ml water
1 teaspoon sea salt
1 teaspoon vegetable oil

Sift the flour into a bowl and make a well in the centre. Add the rest of the
ingredients to the well, then use a wooden spoon to bring the dough together.
Tip out the dough onto a floured bench and knead for 5 minutes or until smooth
and elastic. Wrap in cling film and set aside for 30 minutes to rest.

PORK AND PRAWN FILLING

400 g pork mince
250 g raw prawn meat, roughly chopped
4 fresh shiitake mushrooms, stalks removed,
caps diced
2 tablespoons caster sugar
1½ tablespoons oyster sauce
2 teaspoons sea salt
4 spring onions, finely chopped
1 tablespoon cornflour, plus extra for dusting
pinch of freshly ground white pepper
1 tablespoon sesame oil
1 tablespoon Shaoxing wine
1 egg white

Combine all the ingredients in a bowl. Pick up small balls of the mixture with your
hands and gently slap back into the bowl. Keep doing this for about 3 minutes to
work the filling and create a firm, bouncy texture.

TO FILL AND SHAPE THE SIU MAI

Roll the dough through a pasta machine to a thickness of 1.5 mm. Place lengths of
the dough on a floured bench and cut out rounds about 10 cm in diameter. (You
can stack these floured siu mai wrappers on top of each other and wrap them in
stacks of about 10 for later use: they'll keep for 3–4 days in the fridge, or up to
4 months in the freezer.)

Place a heaped tablespoon of the filling in the middle of a wrapper and gently
gather the rest of the dough around the sides, leaving the top open. Dab the bottom
of the dumpling in a little extra cornflour to prevent it sticking to the steamer.
Repeat with the rest of the wrappers and filling.

TO FINISH

Steam the siu mai in batches in an oiled steamer basket for 6 minutes or until the
filling is cooked through. Serve the dumplings with soy sauce and chilli sauce.

PORK DUMPLINGS
WITH SICHUAN SAUCE

Makes about 20

I love these dumplings, but I suspect it's partly because of the Sichuan sauce
(see page 15) – I'm so addicted to its hot, numbing sensation that I could eat it all day.

DUMPLING DOUGH

500 g (3⅓ cups) plain flour,
plus extra for dusting
250 ml (1 cup) water

Sift the flour into a bowl and pour in the water. Mix with a wooden spoon until a dough forms, then tip out onto a floured bench and knead for 5 minutes or until smooth. Cover with a bowl and leave to rest for 10 minutes.

PORK AND CABBAGE FILLING

500 g pork mince
50 g lap cheong, chopped
50 g salted Tianjin preserved cabbage,
rinsed and chopped
1½ tablespoons peanut oil
1½ tablespoons light soy sauce
60 ml (¼ cup) water
3 cm knob of ginger, finely chopped

Combine all the ingredients in a bowl.

TO FILL AND SHAPE THE DUMPLINGS

Divide the dough into walnut-sized balls and re-cover with the bowl. Use a small rolling pin to roll out a dough ball into a circle about 10 cm in diameter. Place about 2 teaspoons of filling in the middle and fold in half to make a half-moon shape. Pleat the top into a series of folds to seal, then dip the bottom of the dumpling into some flour to prevent it sticking to the frying pan. Repeat with the rest of the dough balls and filling.

TO COOK THE DUMPLINGS

vegetable oil, for pan-frying
about 500 ml (2 cups) Chinese chicken stock
(see page 17) or water, or as needed

Pour a film of oil into a large heavy-based frying pan over medium–high heat. Working in batches, add the dumplings in a single layer, with their pleated side facing up. When they start to sizzle, pour enough chicken stock into the pan to come about a quarter of the way up the sides of the dumplings.

Cover with a lid and reduce the heat to medium. When all the stock has evaporated, the dumplings will sizzle and pop. Remove the lid and cook for a few more minutes or until a crust forms on the bottoms of the dumplings.

TO FINISH

Carefully transfer the dumplings to serving bowls and serve with plenty of the Sichuan sauce.

VEGETABLE DUMPLINGS
WITH SICHUAN SAUCE

Makes about 30

A beautiful, green-hued vegetarian dumpling, served with my favourite sauce,
the Sichuan sauce on page 15, as well as a bowl of pickled green chillies
(see page 15). The dumplings can be frozen prior to cooking.

1 tablespoon vegetable oil
2 carrots, finely diced
150 g fresh shiitake mushrooms, stalks
removed, caps finely diced
150 g pickled mustard greens, finely chopped
1 tablespoon Shaoxing wine
pinch of white sugar
1 tablespoon light soy sauce

VEGETABLE FILLING
Heat the oil in a heavy-based saucepan or wok over medium heat. Add the carrot
and cook for 1 minute, then add the shiitake and cook for another minute. Add the
pickled mustard greens and Shaoxing wine, stirring to deglaze the pan. Cook for
a minute until the alcohol in the wine has cooked out. Stir in the rest of the
ingredients, then set aside to cool.

100 g spinach leaves
300 ml water
500 g (3⅓ cups) plain flour,
plus extra for dusting

DUMPLING DOUGH
Place the spinach in a small saucepan with 150 ml of the water. Bring to the boil,
then remove from the heat, purée and strain the green water into a heatproof
measuring jug, discarding the solids. Sift the flour into a bowl, then pour in 100 ml
of the green water and the remaining water. Mix with a wooden spoon until
a dough forms, then tip out onto a floured bench and knead for 5 minutes or
until smooth. Cover with a bowl and leave to rest for 10 minutes.

TO FILL AND SHAPE THE DUMPLINGS
Divide the rested dough into walnut-sized balls and re-cover with the bowl. Use
a small rolling pin to roll out a dough ball into a round about 10 cm in diameter.
Place about 2 teaspoons of filling in the middle and fold in half to make a half-moon
shape. Pleat the top of the dumpling into a series of folds to seal, then dip the
bottom into some flour to prevent it sticking to the frying pan. Repeat with
the rest of the dough balls and filling.

vegetable oil, for pan-frying
about 500 ml (2 cups) Chinese chicken stock
(see page 17) or water, or as needed

TO COOK THE DUMPLINGS
Pour a film of oil into a large heavy-based frying pan over medium–high heat.
Working in batches, add the dumplings in a single layer, with their pleated side
facing up. When they start to sizzle, pour enough chicken stock into the pan to
come about one quarter of the way up the sides of the dumplings.

Cover with a lid and reduce the heat to medium. When all the stock has
evaporated, the dumplings will sizzle and pop. Remove the lid and cook for a few
more minutes or until a crust forms on the bottoms of the dumplings.

TO FINISH
Carefully transfer the dumplings to serving bowls and serve with plenty of the
Sichuan sauce.

PORK AND CRAB XIAO LONG BAO

Makes about 30

These famous soup dumplings originated in Shanghai but have now found their way around the world. The best approach to eating them is to gingerly bite the side and suck out the steaming-hot soup before eating the rest of the dumpling. The gelatinous superior stock needs to be made the day before, to give it a chance to cool and set properly. You should be able to get all the bones for the stock from your butcher, but you may need to order them in advance. Make sure you get pork mince with at least 25 per cent fat content, or your xiao long bao will be dry.

SUPERIOR STOCK

300 g pork bones
300 g duck bones
300 g chicken wings
300 g pork hock
2.5 litres cold Chinese chicken stock (see page 17)
2 cm knob of ginger, roughly chopped
3 cloves garlic, peeled
150 ml Shaoxing wine
1½ tablespoons yellow rock sugar, crushed

Place the pork bones in a stockpot or large heavy-based saucepan of cold water and bring to the boil. Simmer for 1 minute, then remove the bones and give them a good wash under cold water to get rid of all the impurities. Repeat this process individually with the duck bones, chicken wings and pork hocks. (The cleaner the bones, the clearer your stock will be.) Place all the clean bones in the cleaned-out stockpot, cover with the chicken stock and place over medium–high heat. Skim off any impurities that rise to the surface as the stock is coming to the boil, then turn down to a light simmer and add the rest of the ingredients. Simmer for 4 hours, then strain the stock into a clean stockpot and return to the heat. Keep simmering the stock until it has reduced down to 1 litre. Leave to cool and set overnight in the fridge.

XIAO LONG BAO DOUGH

175 g strong white bread flour
175 g plain flour, plus extra for dusting
125 ml (½ cup) boiling water
60 ml (¼ cup) cold water

Sift the strong flour and plain flour into a bowl. Add the boiling water and mix until big crumbly pieces form, then add the cold water and keep mixing until a dough comes together. Turn out onto a lightly floured bench and knead for 15 minutes or until smooth. Wrap in cling film and leave to rest for 2 hours.

XIAO LONG BAO FILLING

200 g fatty pork mince
60 g raw crab meat
1 small spring onion, finely chopped
1 teaspoon caster sugar
1 tablespoon light soy sauce
½ teaspoon sea salt
¼ teaspoon freshly ground white pepper
3 teaspoons finely chopped ginger
½ teaspoon Shaoxing wine
½ teaspoon sesame oil

Put 750 ml (3 cups) of the gelatinous superior stock into a large bowl. Add the remaining ingredients and mix everything together very well, making sure the stock is evenly distributed.

TO FILL AND SHAPE THE XIAO LONG BAO

Check the consistency of the rested dough: it needs to be quite soft and stretchy. If it seems too firm, knead in a little more water. On a well-floured bench, roll the dough into 4 cm thick logs and cut off 1 cm thick pieces, keeping them covered with a damp tea towel so they don't dry out. To shape the xiao long bao, flatten each piece of dough into a thick disc, then roll into a round about 8 cm in diameter, making them as thin as possible at the edges, and no more than 5 mm thick in the middle. Place a heaped tablespoon of filling in the middle and start pleating the edges of the dough round with your fingers and thumb, squeezing firmly while pulling vertically to stop the centre of the finished dumpling from being too thick and doughy; twist to enclose and form a peak. Repeat with the rest of the dough and filling.

TO FINISH

cabbage leaves, for lining steamer basket

Working in batches, place the xiao long bao in a bamboo steamer lined with cabbage leaves and steam over simmering water for 8 minutes.

STEAMED RICE NOODLE ROLL
WITH CHAR SIU PORK

Makes 4

If you live near a Chinatown, you could make these with 100 g ready-made BBQ
pork and 400 g fresh rice noodles. However, they will be nowhere near as delicate
as homemade noodle sheets – you will be surprised how easy they are to make
once you've had some practice, and there is no end to the fillings you can use.

CHAR SIU PORK

50 g honey
25 ml Shaoxing wine
1 teaspoon fine salt
200 g white sugar
150 g hoisin sauce
25 g fermented red bean curd
3 cloves garlic
150 ml light soy sauce
50 g sweet bean paste
1 teaspoon ground red yeast rice (koji) (optional)
1 star anise
1 cinnamon stick
500 g pork neck, cut lengthways into 10 cm wide strips

Place the honey, Shaoxing wine, salt, sugar, hoisin sauce, fermented red bean curd, garlic, soy sauce, sweet bean paste and red yeast rice, if using, in a blender and blend to a purée. Transfer to a non-reactive bowl and add the star anise, cinnamon and pork. Mix well, then leave to marinate in the fridge for 4–5 hours.

Grill the pork on a baking tray under a very hot grill for 15–20 minutes or until cooked through, basting with the marinade every 3 minutes and turning every 6 minutes.

RICE NOODLES

200 g (1 cup) rice flour
75 g (½ cup) cornflour
750 ml (3 cups) water
1 teaspoon vegetable oil, plus extra for oiling and brushing

Place the rice flour and cornflour in a bowl. Add the water and oil and mix well, then set aside to rest for 15 minutes.

Set up your steamer and choose a heatproof tray or plate that will fit inside the steamer basket. Lightly oil the tray with oil. Stir the batter, as the flour tends to settle on the bottom of the bowl, then pour a very fine layer onto the tray. Steam over simmering water for 8 minutes over medium heat. When it's ready, you should be able to carefully pull the rice noodle off the plate. Repeat this process until all the rice flour mixture is used. As the rice noodles are cooked, stack them on top of each other, brushing each one with oil to prevent sticking. They need to be stored at room temperature and kept wrapped in cling film at all times.

HOISIN SPREADING SAUCE

200 g hoisin sauce
30 g sweet bean paste
2 teaspoons sesame oil
2 teaspoons rice wine vinegar

Whisk all the ingredients together in a bowl until well combined and smooth.

SOY DRESSING

160 ml (⅔ cup) Chinese chicken stock (see page 17)
60 ml (¼ cup) light soy sauce
1½ tablespoons dark soy sauce
50 g white sugar
pinch of freshly ground white pepper
1 teaspoon sesame oil

Bring the chicken stock to the boil in a small heavy-based saucepan. Add the remaining ingredients and simmer for 1 minute, stirring to dissolve the sugar, then keep warm.

TO FINISH

1 Lebanese (small) cucumber, cut into batons
1 fresh red chilli, finely sliced
100 g (⅓ cup) hoisin sauce

Place a rice noodle sheet on a board or plate and smear with about 1 tablespoon of the hoisin spreading sauce. Thinly slice the char siu pork and lay one quarter of it along the middle of the noodle sheet. Top with one quarter of the cucumber and chilli. Roll up the noodle sheet to enclose the filling. Cut each roll crossways into three even pieces and place next to each other in a single layer on a heatproof plate. Steam for 1 minute, then carefully transfer to a bowl and pour over some of the warm soy dressing. Repeat with the remaining ingredients.

BBQ PORK BUNS

Makes about 20

These classic yum cha steamed buns with their rich red pork filling are irresistible.
Making your own dough takes them to another level. You can serve these with
a bowl of fresh chillies in soy sauce and Chinkiang black vinegar to the side.

CHAR SIU MARINADE

50 g honey
25 ml Shaoxing wine
1 teaspoon salt
200 g white sugar
150 g hoisin sauce
25 g fermented red bean curd
3 cloves garlic, peeled
150 ml light soy sauce
50 g sweet bean paste
1 teaspoon ground red yeast rice (koji)
1 star anise
1 cinnamon stick

Place the honey, Shaoxing wine, salt, sugar, hoisin sauce, sweet bean paste, fermented red bean curd, garlic, light soy sauce and red yeast rice in a blender and blend to a purée. Transfer to a non-reactive bowl and add the star anise and cinnamon.

PORK BUN FILLING

600 g pork neck, cut lengthways into 10 cm wide strips
200 g hoisin sauce
2 tablespoons Shaoxing wine
2 tablespoons mushroom soy sauce
1 tablespoon light soy sauce
2 teaspoons dark soy sauce
1 tablespoon peanut oil
200 g golden shallots, finely diced
2 teaspoons ground red yeast rice (koji)
1 tablespoon finely chopped coriander
2 spring onions, finely sliced

Place the pork in the char siu marinade and leave to marinate in the fridge for 4–5 hours. Remove the marinated pork and cut into 1.5 cm dice. Place in a bowl with the rest of the ingredients, then mix well, cover and refrigerate for 1 hour.

BUN DOUGH

500 g (3⅓ cups) Hong Kong flour, plus extra for dusting
1 teaspoon caster sugar
1 teaspoon dried yeast
300 ml tepid water

Sift the flour and sugar into a bowl. Dissolve the yeast in the tepid water, then stir into the dry ingredients with a wooden spoon until a dough forms. Tip out the dough onto a floured bench and knead for 10 minutes or until smooth. Wrap the dough in cling film and leave to rest for 10 minutes.

TO FILL AND SHAPE THE PORK BUNS

Unwrap the dough and punch lightly to knock it back, then knead for another 5 minutes or until smooth and elastic. Divide into golfball-sized balls, keeping them covered with cling film to prevent the dough drying out.

On a floured bench, roll out each ball into a round about 10 cm in diameter. Place 2 tablespoons of the filling in the middle of each round, then bring the edges together and twist to seal at the top. Leave the buns, covered with cling film, in a nice warm spot to prove for 15 minutes or until slightly risen. Place the buns, in batches, in a single layer in a bamboo steamer and steam over boiling water for 12 minutes or until fluffy.

BRAISED EGGPLANT STUFFED
WITH PRAWN AND FLATHEAD

Serves 4–6 as part of a shared meal

I love this combination of meltingly tender eggplant and mousse-like seafood
paste. Capsicums (peppers) can be stuffed and braised the same way. If you happen
to have made any of the pickles on pages 24–28, or the pickled green chillies on
page 15, then serve these in small bowls alongside.

PRAWN AND FLATHEAD FILLING

125 g raw prawn meat, roughly chopped
250 g flathead or other white fish fillets,
finely chopped
1 spring onion, finely sliced
2 cm knob of ginger, finely chopped
2 cloves garlic, finely chopped
2 tablespoons light soy sauce
1 teaspoon white sugar
1 tablespoon Shaoxing wine
2 egg whites

Combine all the ingredients, except the egg whites, in a bowl. In another bowl,
whisk the egg whites until soft peaks form, then gently fold the egg white through
the prawn and flathead mixture. Cover and chill in the fridge for 1 hour to firm up
a little.

TO PREPARE THE EGGPLANT

2 large eggplants (aubergines)
fine salt
cornflour, for dusting
vegetable oil, for deep-frying

Cut the eggplants into 3 cm rounds, then place in a colander set over a plate and
sprinkle lightly with salt. Leave for 15 minutes to draw out any excess moisture,
then rinse and pat dry with paper towel. Lay out the eggplant slices and dust lightly
with cornflour on one side only. Spread a 2 cm layer of the filling on the dusted
side of an eggplant slice, then top with another slice, dusted-side down, to create
a sandwich.

Heat the deep-frying oil to 190°C and deep-fry the stuffed eggplant for
2 minutes or until dark brown, then drain on paper towel. Repeat with the
remaining eggplant slices and filling.

BRAISING LIQUID

400 ml Chinese chicken stock (see page 17)
1½ tablespoons Chinkiang black vinegar
1½ tablespoons light soy sauce
30 g caster sugar
1½ tablespoons oyster sauce

TO BRAISE THE EGGPLANT

Place all the ingredients in a large heavy-based saucepan and bring to the boil. Let
it bubble for 5 minutes, then turn down the heat and keep at a low simmer. Gently
lower the deep-fried eggplant into the braising liquid and cook for 6–8 minutes,
turning a few times so it cooks evenly.

TO FINISH

shredded coriander and finely sliced
spring onion, white part only

Use a slotted spoon or Chinese strainer to lift the stuffed eggplant into a serving
bowl or bowls. Ladle over some of the braising liquid, then garnish with the
coriander and spring onion and serve immediately.

LION'S HEAD MEATBALLS

Serves 4–6 as part of a shared meal

These meatballs are awesome, and you can easily have your butcher mince the
meat for you – remember to ask for fatty pork, so your meatballs stay moist.

650 g pork mince
325 g silken tofu
30 g caster sugar
1½ tablespoons light soy sauce
10 cm knob of ginger, roughly chopped
6 cloves garlic, roughly chopped
25 ml sesame oil
plain flour, for dusting
vegetable oil, for greasing and pan-frying

MEATBALLS

Place all the ingredients, except the flour and vegetable oil, in a bowl and mix with
a wooden spoon until well combined. The mixture is quite delicate and needs to
be worked to give it a firmer texture. You can do this either by putting it through
a mincer three times, beating it for a minute or so in an electric mixer, or repeatedly
picking up small balls of the mixture in your hands and slapping them against the
side of the bowl until the texture firms. Cover with cling film and chill in the fridge
for at least 3 hours.

Roll the chilled meat mixture into golfball-sized balls and place on an oiled tray.
When all the meatballs are made, dust them with a little flour and pan-fry in a heavy-
based frying pan in a film of hot vegetable oil for 15 seconds just to set them.

1 tablespoon vegetable oil
8 cm knob of ginger, cut into fine julienne strips
50 g chilli bean paste
1 tablespoon Shaoxing wine
1 litre Chinese chicken stock (see page 17)
100 ml light soy sauce
40 g caster sugar

TO BRAISE THE MEATBALLS

Heat the oil in a wok over medium heat and fry the ginger until fragrant. Add the
chilli bean paste and fry for another minute, then add the rest of the ingredients
and bring to a simmer, stirring to dissolve the sugar. Slip the lightly fried meatballs
into the sauce and braise gently for 3 minutes or until just cooked through.

chilli oil and finely sliced spring onion

TO SERVE

Transfer the meatballs and braising sauce to a serving bowl and finish with chilli oil
and spring onion.

RADISH CAKES WITH LAP CHEONG, SHIITAKE AND QUAIL EGG

Serves 4–6 as part of a shared meal

Traditionally eaten as a snack, these steamed radish cakes are often pan-fried for extra taste and texture. You would never believe how the unappealing-looking radish paste turns into such a delicious treat. I'm a massive fan, and I tend to like a lot of flavouring through the dough. Serve these with the chilli sauce on page 14.

600 g daikon (long white radish), peeled and grated

fine salt

250 g (2¼ cups) rice flour

2 teaspoons cornflour

1 teaspoon sesame oil

½ teaspoon freshly ground white pepper

1.4 litres water

80 g dried shiitakes, soaked in warm water for 30 minutes, drained and finely diced

50 g lap cheong, finely diced

40 g smoked speck, finely diced

1 teaspoon dried shrimp, soaked in warm water for 30 minutes, drained and chopped

RADISH CAKES

Place the grated daikon in a colander set over a bowl and sprinkle lightly with salt. Leave for 30 minutes to draw out the excess moisture, then rinse well and use your hands to squeeze the daikon as dry as possible. Place the daikon in a saucepan with the rice flour, cornflour, sesame oil, pepper and water. Place over medium heat and stir constantly until the mixture forms a thick dough and becomes slightly translucent – this should take about 20 minutes. Remove from the heat and stir through the shiitake, lap cheong, speck and dried shrimp, then pour into an oiled rectangular baking dish 20 cm by 15 cm. Cover with cling film and steam the radish cake in a large steamer basket for 1 hour. Remove from the steamer and chill in the fridge for at least 3 hours before cutting into 4–5 cm squares.

150 ml red vinegar

60 ml (¼ cup) light soy sauce

1 teaspoon sesame oil

2 tablespoons caster sugar

RED VINEGAR DRESSING

Simply mix all the ingredients together in a small jug or bowl, stirring until the sugar has dissolved.

2 tablespoons vegetable oil

8 quail eggs

coriander leaves, finely sliced spring onion, and chilli sauce

TO FINISH

Heat the oil in a large heavy-based frying pan and fry the radish cake squares until the outside is crisp and the inside is hot. Crack the quail eggs into the pan and scramble lightly. Transfer the radish cake and egg to a serving plate, pour over a generous amount of red vinegar dressing and garnish with coriander, spring onion and a spoonful of chilli sauce. Serve immediately.

EGG CUSTARD WITH CRAB AND XO SAUCE

Serves 4 as part of a shared meal

Inspired by the Chinese tradition of eating steamed custards with spicy food,
we added a luscious crab and XO topping to make this beautifully textured dish.
This is one of the easiest yum cha offerings to make at home, and is well worth
trying. It's also amazing spooned over steamed rice for a light meal.

EGG CUSTARD

8 eggs
80 ml (⅓ cup) Chinese chicken stock (see page 17)

Mix the eggs and stock together in a bowl, then strain into a clean bowl or jug. Divide the custard mixture evenly among four heatproof bowls about 15–20 cm in diameter and 10 cm deep. Cover with cling film and lightly steam for 15–20 minutes or until the egg is just set, but not too firm.

CRAB AND XO SAUCE

peanut oil, for frying
80 ml (⅓ cup) XO sauce (see page 14)
1 tablespoon light soy sauce
1 tablespoon caster sugar
200 g raw spanner crab meat

Heat a little oil in a wok over low heat, add the XO sauce and fry for 30 seconds or until fragrant. Season with the soy sauce and sugar, then add the crab meat and gently poach until just cooked.

TO FINISH

finely sliced spring onion, white part only

Spoon the crab and XO sauce evenly on top of the steamed custards, garnish with spring onion and serve immediately.

GUA BAO

Makes about 30

These little steamed buns have been a street food in China for a thousand years.
And for good reason – they are totally addictive. Filled with Spice Temple's
braised or roasted meats, or any of the salads in this book (pictured overleaf),
or they make perfect cocktail food. Any leftover unfilled gua bao can be
frozen for up to six months.

1 kg Hong Kong flour, plus extra for dusting
12 g dried yeast
35 g caster sugar
650 ml tepid water, plus extra if needed

Place all the ingredients in a large bowl. Use your hands to bring the dough together, adding a little more water if needed, then transfer to a floured bench and knead for 15–20 minutes or until the dough forms a smooth ball. Put the dough into a clean bowl, cover and leave to rise in a warm place for 1 hour or until doubled in size.

Unwrap the dough and divide into golfball-sized balls. Place each ball of dough on a round of baking paper to prevent sticking to the steamer basket. Cover with a clean tea towel and leave to rise in a warm place for 30 minutes.

Transfer the risen gua bao to a large metal or bamboo steamer basket, spacing them about 2 cm apart. Steam in batches over simmering water over medium heat for 10 minutes or until springy to the touch.

Cut in half, add your choice of filling (see pages 63 and 67) and serve warm.

GUA BAO WITH CHAR SIU PORK
AND HOISIN SAUCE

Makes 1

1 gua bao (see opposite)
1 tablespoon hoisin sauce
50 g char siu pork (see page 51), sliced
2 slices pickled cucumber (see page 17)
1 tablespoon roasted unsalted peanuts, crushed

Slice the warm gua bao in half, then smear the hoisin sauce on the bottom half. Add the char siu pork, followed by the pickled cucumber and the peanuts, then top with the other half of the bun.

GUA BAO WITH RED-BRAISED LAMB SHOULDER
AND CHILLI PASTE

Makes 1

1 gua bao (see opposite)
1 teaspoon dark chilli paste (see page 15)
30 g red-braised lamb shoulder, shredded
(see page 20)
1 teaspoon pickled mustard greens, sliced
1 teaspoon sweet peanuts (½ teaspoon crushed
roasted unsalted peanuts mixed with
½ teaspoon crushed yellow rock sugar)

Slice the warm gua bao in half, then smear the chilli paste on the bottom half. Add the shredded lamb, followed by the mustard greens and peanuts, then top with the other half of the bun.

GUA BAO WITH WHITE-CUT CHICKEN,
SALTED CHILLIES AND PICKLES

Makes 1

1 gua bao (see opposite)
30 g salted chillies (see page 15), or to taste
30 g breast of white-cut chicken
(see page 18), shredded
2 teaspoons ginger and spring onion dressing
(see page 179)
2 slices pickled cucumber (see page 17)

Slice the warm gua bao in half, then smear the salted chillies on the bottom half. Toss the chicken through the dressing and place in the bun, then top with the pickled cucumber and the top half of the bun.

CRISPY GUANGXI
PORK BELLY SLIDER

Makes 1

The softness of the gua bao is complemented by the rich crispness
of the pork belly and tangy crunch of the pickles.

ONION AND PEANUT SALAD

1 small spring onion, cut into fine julienne strips

1 very fine slice red onion

couple of coriander leaves

2 slices pickled cucumber (see page 17)

1 teaspoon crushed roasted unsalted peanuts

1 teaspoon Chinkiang black vinegar

1 teaspoon peanut oil

Place all the ingredients in a small bowl and toss together.

TO ASSEMBLE

1 gua bao (see page 62)

½ teaspoon salted chillies (see page 15)

30 g crispy pork belly (see page 21), sliced

2 teaspoons mustard dressing (see page 80)

Slice the warm gua bao in half, then smear the salted chillies on the bottom half. Add the pork belly, followed by the onion and peanut salad and drizzle over the mustard dressing, then top with the other half of the bun.

SALADS AND COLD CUTS

AROMATIC DUCK SALAD WITH TEA EGGS AND CORIANDER

Serves 4–6 as part of a shared meal

This is a great blend of flavours and textures, with the meatiness of the duck perfectly complementing the creamy yolk of the hard-boiled tea egg.

200 g red-braised duck (see page 20)
1 tea egg (see page 21), cut into 6 wedges
handful of coriander leaves
20 g crushed roasted unsalted peanuts
¼ teaspoon chilli flakes
3 teaspoons Chinkiang black vinegar
1 teaspoon dark soy sauce
2 teaspoons sesame oil
3 teaspoons chilli oil
finely sliced small red chilli, to serve

Slice the duck and place in a large bowl, add the remaining ingredients, then toss gently to combine.

Serve the salad in a beautiful shallow bowl or on a plate.

SPINACH AND SESAME SALAD

Serves 4–6 as part of a shared meal

This simple salad is all about the earthiness of spinach and the
nutty taste and aroma of sesame oil.

500 g spinach
fine salt
1½ tablespoons peanut oil
6 dried long red chillies
3 teaspoons caster sugar
2 teaspoons rice wine vinegar
½ teaspoon sesame oil
½ teaspoon light soy sauce
½ teaspoon chilli oil
roasted sesame seeds, to serve

Plunge the spinach into a saucepan of boiling salted water and blanch for a minute, just to wilt the leaves. Refresh under cold running water and squeeze dry.

Heat a wok over high heat until smoking and add the peanut oil. Reduce the heat to medium and briefly stir-fry the chillies for 10 seconds or until fragrant, then remove from the wok and set aside.

In a large bowl, mix together the rest of the ingredients. Add the blanched spinach and fried chillies to the bowl, mix together gently and scatter with sesame seeds, then serve.

STEAMED EGGPLANT WITH THREE FLAVOURS: GARLIC, CORIANDER AND SWEET PORK

Serves 4–6 as part of a shared meal

When I first encountered this dish at a Jiangxi restaurant in Beijing, I loved the drama of watching the waiter fold the three-coloured topping of creamy white garlic, green coriander and sweet red-brown meat through the silky steamed eggplant.

½ eggplant (aubergine), peeled and cut into batons
1 tablespoon sea salt
8 cloves garlic, peeled
1½ tablespoons peanut oil
100 g pork mince
1½ tablespoons sweet bean paste
1 tablespoon dark soy sauce
100 ml Chinese chicken stock (see page 17)
½ teaspoon sesame oil
large handful of finely shredded coriander

Toss the eggplant and salt together in a large bowl and set aside for 1 hour. Rinse the eggplant, draining it well, then place in a steamer basket and steam over simmering water for 14 minutes.

Add the garlic cloves to a small saucepan of boiling water and blanch for 1 minute or until soft, then drain and finely chop the garlic.

Heat a wok over high heat until smoking hot and add the peanut oil. Stir-fry the pork mince for 30 seconds or until just coloured, then remove from the wok. Add the sweet bean paste to the wok and stir-fry until it loses its raw smell and taste, then return the pork to the wok, along with the soy sauce and chicken stock. Stir-fry until the sauce thickens slightly, then remove from the heat and stir through the sesame oil.

Place the steamed eggplant on a plate. Cover one-third with chopped coriander, one-third with the pork sauce and the remaining third with the chopped garlic.

TINGLING PRAWNS

Serves 4–6 as part of a shared meal

On our research trip to China, we sampled delicious salads and dressings from
Hunan, Sichuan, Yunnan and Jiangxi – but most of them included shredded
chicken. So one of our challenges was to reinterpret those ideas, but not end
up with a menu full of chicken dishes! And so this prawn salad was born,
with Sichuan peppercorns and a little green chilli to get the tastebuds tingling.

3 fresh long green chillies, seeds removed,
finely diced
3 cm knob of ginger, finely chopped
handful of coriander, leaves picked,
stems roughly chopped
pinch of sea salt
½ teaspoon caster sugar
2 pinches of roasted and ground Sichuan
pepper (see page 17)
1 tablespoon rice wine vinegar
90 ml spring onion oil (see page 17)
300 g cooked king prawns in the shell,
peeled and deveined
3 spring onions, cut on the diagonal
into 5 cm lengths

Place the green chilli, ginger, coriander stems, sea salt, sugar and a pinch of the Sichuan
pepper in a mortar. Pound to a paste with the pestle, then stir in the vinegar and spring
onion oil to make a dressing.

Place the prawns in a bowl with the coriander leaves and spring onion. Pour
over the dressing and mix well, then transfer to a plate and sprinkle over another
pinch of Sichuan pepper.

BANG-BANG CHICKEN

Serves 4–6 as part of a shared meal

This evocatively named dish is a Sichuanese classic, so called for the banging and clanging of the street vendors' knife blades as they sharpen them to shred the chicken meat. The dressing is also dubbed 'strange flavour', as the Sichuanese consider the black vinegar and sesame paste a strange combination that shouldn't taste good – but it does. I like this really hot.

2 litres water
150 ml Shaoxing wine
40 g (⅓ cup) sea salt
3 cm knob of ginger, bruised
3 cloves garlic, smashed
4 spring onions, bruised
1 chicken leg and thigh portion

TO COOK THE CHICKEN

Place all the ingredients, except the chicken, in a medium heavy-based saucepan and bring to the boil. Add the chicken to the boiling stock, then reduce to a simmer and cook gently for 12 minutes. Take the pan off the heat and leave the chicken to steep in the stock for 2 hours, then remove from the stock and leave to cool to room temperature.

55 g (¼ cup) caster sugar
60 ml (¼ cup) light soy sauce
60 ml (¼ cup) Chinkiang black vinegar
70 g Chinese sesame seed paste
1 teaspoon sesame oil
100 ml Chinese chicken stock (see page 17)
50 ml chilli oil

DRESSING

Simply whisk all the dressing ingredients together in a bowl until well combined.

¼ Lebanese (small) cucumber, cut into fine julienne strips
30 g bean sprouts, trimmed
1 teaspoon roasted and ground Sichuan pepper (see page 17)
3 teaspoons roasted sesame seeds
1 teaspoon chilli flakes
1 tablespoon coriander leaves

TO FINISH

Shred the meat from the chicken leg, discarding the bones. Place the cucumber, bean sprouts and chicken in a bowl, then pour the dressing liberally over. Garnish with the Sichuan pepper, sesame seeds, chilli flakes and coriander leaves, tossing gently to mix. Transfer to a serving dish, then serve.

TEA-SMOKED DUCK BREAST
WITH PICKLED CABBAGE
AND MUSTARD DRESSING

Serves 4–6 as part of a shared meal

For this brilliant dish, the duck breast is first brined to cure it and then smoked.
The end result is tender, smoky duck with a crunchy cabbage pickle that is
completely addictive. The pickled cabbage will need to be made in advance,
as it needs to pickle in the fridge overnight.

PICKLED CABBAGE

5 leaves Chinese cabbage (wombok), shredded
3 teaspoons sea salt
150 g (⅔ cup) caster sugar
150 ml white vinegar

Place the cabbage in a bowl with the salt. Mix well, then set aside for 1 hour. Meanwhile, place the sugar and vinegar in a small non-reactive saucepan and bring to the boil, then simmer until reduced by half. Remove from the heat and leave to cool.

Rinse the salted cabbage and drain well. Place in a bowl with the reduced sugar and vinegar mixture, mix well, then cover and leave to pickle in the fridge overnight.

TO COOK THE DUCK BREAST

1 litre water
40 g (⅓ cup) sea salt
1 tablespoon Sichuan peppercorns, roasted until fragrant
10 cm knob of ginger, bruised
4 cloves garlic, bruised
1 duck breast, skin on, trimmed of excess fat

Place all the ingredients, except the duck breast, in a heavy-based saucepan and bring to the boil. Add the duck breast to the pan, then remove from the heat and leave to steep in the fridge for 18 hours. Take the duck out of the stock and drain on paper towel.

TO TEA-SMOKE THE DUCK BREAST

150 g (1 cup) tea-smoking mixture (see page 21)

Make a shallow bowl from foil and place it in the base of a wok, then put the tea-smoking mixture inside. Set a wire rack over the top to hold the duck breast about 5 cm above the smoking mixture (if necessary, use some foil balls to elevate the rack) and cover tightly with a lid. Heat the smoking mixture in the wok over high heat until it starts to smoke, then briefly lift the lid off the wok and place the duck breast on the rack. Replace the lid and smoke the duck breast over high heat for 12 minutes, then turn off the heat and leave the duck to smoke for a further 3 minutes.

MUSTARD DRESSING

1 tablespoon Dijon mustard
3 teaspoons light soy sauce
3 teaspoons white vinegar

Simply whisk all the ingredients together until emulsified.

TO SERVE

Finely slice the tea-smoked duck breast and arrange on a beautiful plate. Drizzle with the mustard dressing and serve with the pickled cabbage spooned on top.

CRISPY PORK BELLY AND SMOKED TOFU WITH SPICY GINGER AND GARLIC DRESSING

Serves 4–6 as part of a shared meal

A great combination of tastes and textures, this salad is brought to life by a classic Sichuan ginger and garlic dressing that's also known as 'fish fragrant dressing', because it was traditionally served with fish.

1 tablespoon peanut oil
2 teaspoons chilli oil
2 teaspoons sesame oil
1 tablespoon light soy sauce
4 cloves garlic, finely chopped
2 cm knob of ginger, finely chopped
50 g pickled green chillies (see page 15), finely chopped, plus 50 ml of their pickling liquid
100 g crispy pork belly (see page 21), finely sliced
30 g fresh black fungi, cut into julienne strips
60 g smoked tofu, finely sliced
3 spring onions, cut on the diagonal into fine julienne strips

In a large bowl, whisk together the peanut oil, chilli oil, sesame oil, soy sauce, garlic, ginger, pickled green chillies and their liquid.

Add the rest of the ingredients and gently toss everything together.

To serve, simply transfer to a beautiful serving platter or bowl.

SILKEN TOFU AND PRESERVED EGGS WITH SOY CHILLI DRESSING

Serves 4–6 as part of a shared meal

In this striking-looking dish, the unique texture and taste of preserved egg contrasts with soft, silky tofu. A soy sauce-based dressing, full of herbs and chillies, lifts the flavours.

PRESERVED EGGS

2 preserved eggs

Place the preserved eggs in a small saucepan, cover with cold water and bring to the boil. Simmer for 12 minutes, then drain and refresh under cold running water.

SOY CHILLI DRESSING

70 ml light soy sauce
50 ml Chinese chicken stock (see page 17)
25 g white sugar
1 tablespoon peanut oil
2 teaspoons sesame oil
6 coriander roots, scraped and rinsed well, then finely sliced
10 coriander stems, finely sliced
1 red shallot, cut in half and finely sliced
2 spring onions, finely sliced
1 fresh long red chill, finely sliced on the diagonal
2 cm knob of ginger, cut into fine julienne strips

Combine the soy sauce, stock, sugar and both oils in a medium-sized bowl and whisk until the sugar has dissolved. Add the rest of the ingredients and mix well.

TO FINISH

1 × 300 g block silken tofu
½ teaspoon roasted and ground Sichuan pepper (see page 17)

Cut the tofu in half lengthways, then cut each half into 4 pieces to give you 8 cubes. Peel the preserved eggs and cut into wedges. Place the tofu in a serving bowl and arrange the egg wedges on top. Spoon the dressing over and around, sprinkle with the Sichuan pepper and serve.

SILKEN TOFU WITH PRESERVED EGG, PORK FLOSS AND SPRING ONION OIL

Serves 4–6 as part of a shared meal

A cooling version of the previous recipe (see page 84), this time with salty pork floss, a vibrant green spring onion oil and no chilli.

PORK FLOSS

50 ml vegetable oil
40 g boneless pork loin

Place a wok over low heat and add the vegetable oil. Heat the oil to 80°C, then adjust the heat to keep it around this temperature – you want to cook the pork at a consistent low temperature. Add the pork loin and fry slowly and steadily for 2 hours, keeping an eye on it during this time. Once all the moisture has evaporated (there will be no more steam, and the pork should be golden brown), remove the pork from the oil and drain well on paper towel. When the pork is cool, blitz it in a blender to create a 'floss' texture.

TO STEAM THE PRESERVED EGG AND TOFU

1 preserved egg
300 g silken tofu

Set a steamer basket over a saucepan or wok of simmering water, then steam the preserved egg for 10 minutes. Remove and refresh under cold running water, then peel and cut into wedges. Place the silken tofu in the steamer for 2–3 minutes, just to warm it through. Cut the tofu in half lengthways, then each half into 4 pieces to give you 8 cubes.

TO FINISH

2 teaspoons deep-fried shallots (see page 21)
2½ teaspoons rice wine vinegar
pinch of sea salt
60 ml (¼ cup) spring onion oil (see page 17)

Place the tofu cubes on a serving plate, along with the preserved egg, pork floss and deep-fried shallots. Stir the vinegar and salt into the spring onion oil, then pour into a bowl and serve on the side.

SHREDDED RED-BRAISED LAMB SHOULDER WITH SALTED CHILLIES

Serves 4–6 as part of a shared meal

This is based on a poached chicken dish we ate at a Hunanese restaurant during our research trip to China, but using deeply flavoured red-braised lamb instead to match the strength and intensity of the salted chilli.

1½ tablespoons peanut oil
1 teaspoon sesame oil
60 ml (¼ cup) Chinese chicken stock (see page 17)
1½ tablespoons light soy sauce
1 teaspoon white sugar
1 teaspoon rice wine vinegar
3 spring onions, finely sliced
2 teaspoons salted chillies (see page 15)

SALTED CHILLI DRESSING
Combine all the ingredients in a bowl. (Alternatively, combine all the ingredients, except the chillies, in a bowl, then top with the chillies before serving.)

200 g red-braised lamb shoulder (see page 20), shredded

TO SERVE
Place the shredded lamb on a serving plate and pour the dressing over the top, then top with the salted chillies.

SHAANXI WHITE-CUT CHICKEN WITH BLACK BEAN AND SESAME DRESSING

Serves 4–6 as part of a shared meal

Food from the Shaanxi region typically involves a lot of hearty, spicy, aromatic flavours, and this salad is no exception.

1½ tablespoons vegetable oil
2 teaspoons finely grated ginger
2 teaspoons finely grated garlic
50 g (⅓ cup) black sesame seeds, soaked overnight in cold water, drained
50 g salted Chinese olives
50 g fermented black beans
60 g Chinese sesame seed paste
2 tablespoons Chinkiang black vinegar
2 tablespoons dark soy sauce
2 tablespoons sesame oil
2 tablespoons chilli oil

BLACK BEAN AND SESAME DRESSING

Heat a wok over low–medium heat and add the vegetable oil. Add the ginger and garlic and fry gently until fragrant and just starting to colour. Add the sesame seeds, olives, black beans and sesame paste and turn the heat down to low, then cook for 30 minutes, stirring regularly. Leave to cool slightly, then transfer to a blender or food processor and blend until smooth. Press through a fine sieve into a bowl and whisk in the rest of the ingredients.

1 litre water
100 g yellow rock sugar, crushed
2 tablespoons sea salt
250 ml (1 cup) Shaoxing wine
5 cm knob of ginger, smashed
5 cloves garlic, smashed
small handful of spring onion tops
1 chicken breast fillet, trimmed of excess sinew

WHITE-CUT CHICKEN BREAST

Place all the ingredients, except the chicken breast, in a large heavy-based saucepan and bring to the boil. Taste for seasoning and adjust accordingly. Return the stock to the boil and add the chicken breast, then immediately turn the heat down to very low and poach the chicken at the gentlest simmer for 12 minutes. Remove the pan from the heat and sit on a wire rack for the chicken to steep and the stock to cool for 15 minutes. Remove the chicken breast from the stock and place on a plate in the fridge to chill.

pickled vegetables, such as cabbage and radish (see page 24) and/or cucumber (see page 17), to serve

TO FINISH

Shred the chicken breast and combine with the dressing, then place on a platter with the pickled vegetables and serve.

AROMATIC CRISPY PORK BELLY WITH TEA EGG AND SALTED CHILLI

Serves 4–6 as part of a shared meal

This is a conglomeration of ingredients from across China, including salted chillies from the south-western province of Yunnan, and tea eggs from Beijing and Shanghai. Crispy pork belly is a favourite everywhere.

2 tablespoons vegetable oil
1 clove garlic, finely chopped
1 cm knob of ginger, finely chopped
1 tablespoon salted chillies (see page 15)
1½ tablespoons mushroom soy sauce
2 tablespoons pickling liquid from pickled green chillies (see page 15) or
1 tablespoon caster sugar, dissolved in 1 tablespoon white vinegar
2 teaspoons sesame oil

DRESSING

Place a wok over low heat and add the vegetable oil. Add the garlic and ginger and cook gently without colouring for 2–3 minutes or until tender and sweet. Remove from the heat and stir in the rest of the ingredients. (Leftover dressing can be stored in an airtight container in the fridge for up to 1 month, and is particularly good with rice, noodles or tofu.)

200 g crispy pork belly (see page 21)
1 tea egg (see page 21), cut into 8 wedges
1 stalk celery, sliced on the diagonal

TO FINISH

Cut the pork belly into bite-sized pieces and place in a bowl with the tea egg, celery and enough of the dressing to just coat them. Gently toss everything together, then transfer to a serving plate and serve.

PRAWN, PICKLED DAIKON AND SMOKED TOFU SALAD WITH GINGER AND LEMON DRESSING

Serves 4–6 as part of a shared meal

The inspiration for this salad came from the city of Hangzhou in eastern China. Flavour profiles from Hangzhou are typically very clean and bright, hence the use of ginger and lemon, but no chilli. You could use ready-made smoked tofu here, if you like. Just remember to start the daikon the day before, as it needs to be left for at least 24 hours to pickle. Leftover pickled daikon will keep indefinitely in the fridge, and is great served alongside rich meat dishes.

PICKLED DAIKON

150 g daikon (long white radish)
100 g caster sugar
100 ml rice wine vinegar

Peel the daikon and cut into strips about 5 cm long and 1 cm wide. Place the sugar and vinegar in a non-reactive bowl and stir to dissolve the sugar. Add the daikon and mix well, then cover and leave in the fridge to pickle for at least 24 hours.

SMOKED TOFU

100 g tea-smoking mixture (see page 21)
250 g five-spice firm tofu

Make a shallow bowl from foil and place it in the base of a wok, then put half of the tea-smoking mixture inside. Set a wire rack over the top to hold the tofu about 5 cm above the smoking mixture (if necessary, use some foil balls to elevate the rack) and cover tightly with a lid. Heat the smoking mixture in the wok over high heat until it starts to smoke, then briefly lift the lid off the wok and place the tofu on the rack. Replace the lid and smoke the tofu over high heat for 5 minutes, then turn off the heat and leave the tofu to smoke for a further 3–7 minutes, depending on how intense you want the smoke flavour to be.

GINGER AND LEMON DRESSING

5 cm knob of ginger, roughly chopped
1 tablespoon rice wine vinegar
2 teaspoons caster sugar
pinch of finely grated lemon zest
few drops of sesame oil

Place the ginger and vinegar in a blender and blend until smooth, then strain through a fine sieve into a bowl. Add the sugar and stir to dissolve, then add the lemon zest and sesame oil.

TO COOK THE PRAWNS

fine salt
8 large raw king prawns
ice

Bring a saucepan of salted water to the boil, drop in the prawns and cook for 2–3 minutes until they just change colour. Drain the prawns, then briefly plunge into a bowl of iced water to arrest the cooking.

TO FINISH

pinch of sea salt
1 spring onion, finely sliced on the diagonal

Peel and devein the prawns, then place in a large bowl. Add half of the pickled daikon, 4 slices of smoked tofu and a tablespoon of the dressing, along with a pinch of salt. Gently toss everything together, then arrange on a beautiful platter. Top with the spring onion and serve.

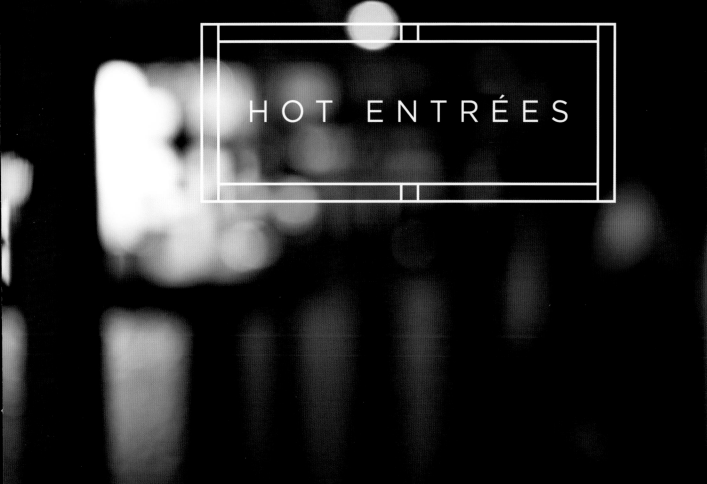

HOT ENTRÉES

SALT AND PEPPER SILKEN TOFU WITH SPICY CORIANDER SALAD

Serves 4–6 as part of a shared meal

This dish is all about the crisp crust and pillowy-soft interior of the warm tofu.
The salad is really quite spicy, so tone it down by using less chilli if you want.
You could even leave out the salad altogether – the fried tofu is killer with just
lemon or lime juice squeezed over.

SPICY CORIANDER SALAD

100 g salted chillies (see page 15)
25 ml rice wine vinegar
1 clove garlic, finely chopped
1 cm knob of ginger, finely chopped
2 teaspoons chilli oil
2 teaspoons sesame oil
2 tablespoons coriander leaves,
finely shredded

Place all the ingredients in a small bowl and toss everything together.

SALT AND PEPPER SILKEN TOFU

50 g (⅓ cup) plain flour
2 teaspoons roasted and ground Sichuan
pepper (see page 17)
1 teaspoon fine salt
1 × 300 g block silken tofu, cut into
3 cm × 2 cm pieces
vegetable oil, for deep-frying

In a wide shallow bowl, mix the flour with the Sichuan pepper and the salt. Dust
the tofu with the seasoned flour, letting it sit in the bowl for about a minute so it
gets a good coating.

Heat the deep-frying oil to 180°C. Working in batches, deep-fry the tofu until
golden, then drain well on paper towel.

TO SERVE

Spoon the salad onto a serving plate, then arrange the tofu on top and serve
immediately.

FISH FRAGRANT EGGPLANT

Serves 4–6 as part of a shared meal

A textural dish that somehow manages to be crunchy, soft and tender all
at the same time. Traditionally, this hot, salty and sharp dressing was served
with steamed or fried fish in Sichuan – and the name stuck.

---

400 g eggplant (aubergine), peeled and cut into 8 cm × 2 cm strips
2 tablespoons fine salt

TO SALT THE EGGPLANT

Place the eggplant strips in a colander set over a plate and sprinkle lightly with salt.
Leave for 30 minutes to draw out any excess moisture, then rinse and pat dry with
paper towel.

250 ml (1 cup) water
45 g rice flour
45 g tapioca flour
½ teaspoon sea salt

BATTER

Whisk all the ingredients together in a large bowl until smooth.

vegetable oil, for deep-frying

TO COOK THE EGGPLANT

Heat the deep-frying oil to 180°C. Working in batches, lightly coat the eggplant
strips in batter, then place, one at a time, in the hot oil and deep-fry for 4 minutes,
or until golden. Drain on paper towel.

2 cm knob of ginger, finely chopped
2 cloves garlic, finely chopped
2 teaspoons chilli oil
2 teaspoons sesame oil
1 tablespoon light soy sauce
1 tablespoon peanut oil
50 g pickled green chillies (see page 15), finely chopped, plus 50 ml of their pickling liquid

FISH FRAGRANT DRESSING

Simply whisk together all the dressing ingredients in a large bowl.

1 spring onion, finely sliced

TO SERVE

Transfer the deep-fried eggplant to a bowl with the dressing and gently toss
together, then arrange on a serving plate. Scatter over the spring onion and serve.

DEEP-FRIED SQUID
WITH HEAVEN-FACING CHILLIES
AND CABBAGE SALAD

Serves 4–6 as part of a shared meal

The rounded heat and wonderful fragrance of heaven-facing chillies enhance
this crispy squid, and the cabbage salad provides a refreshing contrast.

HEAVEN-FACING CHILLIES

200 g heaven-facing chillies
50 ml vegetable oil
2 cm knob of ginger, finely chopped
3 cloves garlic, finely chopped
100 g white sugar
100 g fine salt
100 g (⅔ cup) plain flour

Preheat the oven to its lowest possible setting and prop the door ajar slightly if the lowest temperature is much above 50°C. Spread out the heaven-facing chillies on a baking tray and leave to dry in the oven overnight.

Heat a heavy-based frying pan over medium heat and dry-roast the heaven-facing chillies until they have darkened slightly – keep a close eye on them, as they can quickly burn.

Heat the oil in a wok over low heat and stir-fry the ginger and garlic until lightly golden. Add the heaven-facing chillies and stir-fry for 20 minutes or until fragrant and toasty, then leave to cool slightly. Blitz in a food processor with the sugar and salt until the texture is like fine salt. Tip 1 tablespoon of the ground chilli powder into a wide shallow bowl and stir in the flour. Store the remaining chilli powder in an airtight container for up to 3 months.

CABBAGE SALAD

60 g Chinese cabbage (wombok), finely shredded
1 teaspoon finely shredded coriander
1 teaspoon Chinkiang black vinegar
1 teaspoon peanut oil
1 teaspoon lime juice

Combine all the ingredients in a bowl and toss together.

DEEP-FRIED SQUID

350 g squid, cleaned
vegetable oil, for deep-frying

Cut the squid hood into 2 cm squares and the tentacles into 3 cm lengths. Heat the deep-frying oil to 180°C. Working in batches, dust the squid with the seasoned flour and deep-fry for 2 minutes or until golden and cooked through. Drain on paper towel.

TO SERVE

lime wedges

Place the squid on a platter with the cabbage salad on the side. Serve with lime wedges.

CRISP-FRIED MARINATED QUAIL WITH FERMENTED BEAN CURD AND FIVE SPICE

Serves 4–6 as part of a shared meal

I have always been crazy in love with fermented bean curd. Its pungent, cheese-like flavour adds a richness and depth to the marinade for these quail. This dish is one to eat with your fingers – and although we fry the quail here, they are also amazing barbecued. For the best results, refrigerate the cooked quail in the master stock for 24 hours, then marinate in the marinade for 12–24 hours before deep-frying.

1 litre master stock (see page 18)
2 star anise
4 cloves
1 cinnamon stick
1 teaspoon Sichuan peppercorns
zest of ½ orange, peeled in long strips
2 × 100 g quail, wings and backbone removed

TO COOK THE QUAIL
Place all the ingredients, except the quail, in a large heavy-based saucepan and bring to the boil. Turn off the heat, add the quail to the stock and leave to steep, uncovered, until the stock is cool. If you have time, refrigerate the quail in the stock for 24 hours to infuse it with more flavour.

300 g fermented red bean curd
1½ tablespoons dark soy sauce
1½ tablespoons Shaoxing wine
2 teaspoons five-spice powder

FERMENTED BEAN CURD AND FIVE SPICE MARINADE
Whisk all the ingredients together in a large bowl until smooth. Take the quail out of the stock, add to the marinade and mix well, then leave to marinate in the fridge for 12–24 hours.

vegetable oil, for deep-frying
plain flour, for dusting

TO FRY THE QUAIL
Heat the deep-frying oil to 170°C. Remove the quail from the marinade, dust with flour and deep-fry for 3–4 minutes or until deep golden and cooked through. Drain on paper towel.

coriander leaves and a lemon half

TO SERVE
Place the quail on a serving plate, garnish with coriander leaves and serve with a lemon half.

CARAMELISED AND SMOKED PORK SPARE RIBS

Serves 4–6 as part of a shared meal

These ribs are addictive: smoky, meaty and sweet all at the same time.

---

500 g pork ribs, cut into individual ribs
4 litres cold water
2 tablespoons sea salt
4 cm knob of ginger, bruised
5 cloves garlic, lightly crushed
4 spring onions, bruised

TO BLANCH THE PORK RIBS

Place all the ingredients in a stockpot or large heavy-based saucepan and bring to the boil, then simmer for 5 minutes. Stir well, then remove the pork and rinse well to get rid of any impurities. Leave to cool in the liquid to room temperature.

250 g tea-smoking mixture (see page 21)

TO SMOKE THE PORK RIBS

Make a shallow bowl from foil and place it in the base of a wok, then put the tea-smoking mixture inside. Set a wire rack over the top to hold the pork ribs about 5 cm above the smoking mixture (if necessary, use some foil balls to elevate the rack) and cover tightly with a lid. Heat the smoking mixture in the wok over high heat until it starts to smoke, then briefly lift the lid off the wok and place the pork on the rack. Replace the lid and smoke the pork ribs over high heat for 5 minutes, then turn off the heat and leave the pork ribs to smoke for a further 3–7 minutes, depending on how intense you want the smoke flavour to be.

1½ tablespoons peanut oil
2 cm knob of ginger, finely chopped
2 cloves garlic, finely chopped
50 g white sugar
100 ml Chinkiang black vinegar
1 tablespoon dark soy sauce
3 teaspoons Chinese chicken stock
(see page 17)

SAUCE

Heat the oil in a wok over medium heat and stir-fry the ginger and garlic until fragrant. Add the sugar and caramelise until deep golden brown, then quickly arrest the cooking by adding the rest of the ingredients. Simmer until the sauce has reduced to the consistency of thin cream, then add the smoked ribs and turn in the sauce until coated and glossy.

sea salt, sesame oil and sesame seeds

TO SERVE

Place the pork ribs on a serving plate and finish with sea salt, sesame oil and sesame seeds.

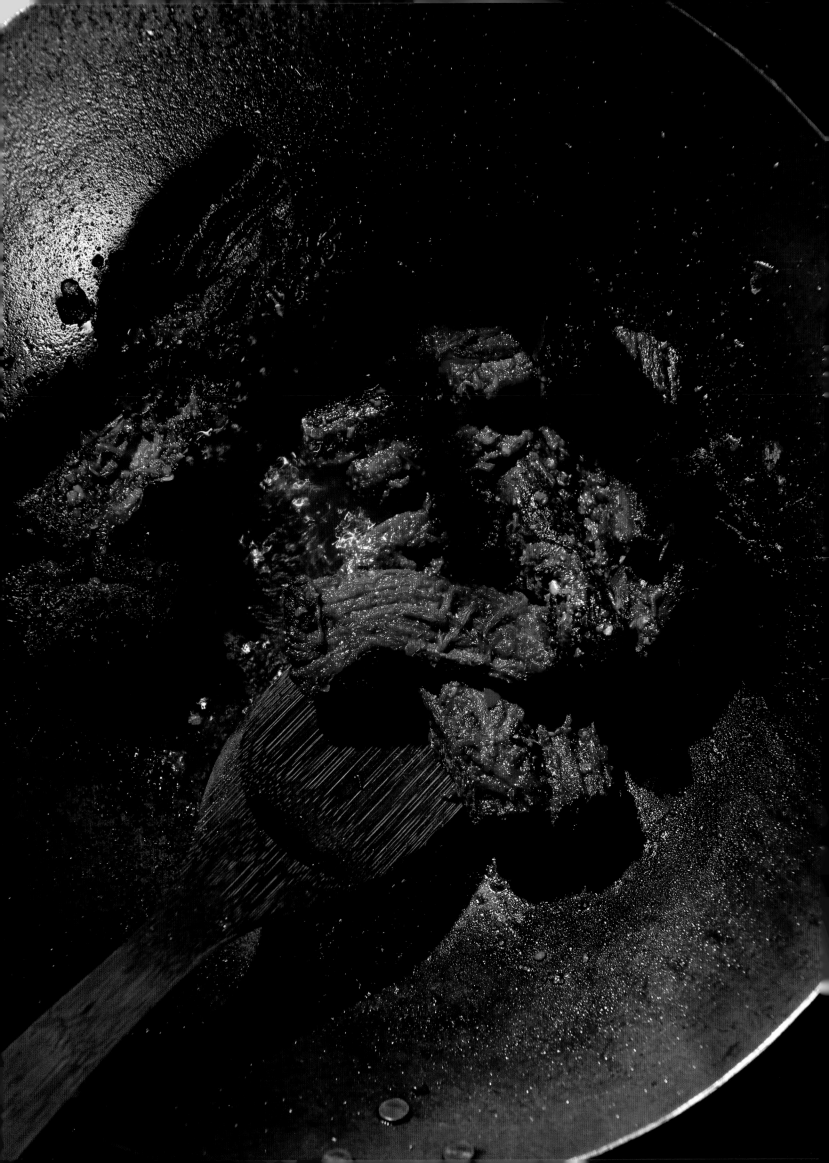

HOT AND NUMBING DRIED BEEF

Serves 4–6 as part of a shared meal

A classic Sichuanese dish that uses several cooking methods to create layers of flavour and texture: braising to render the meat tender; deep-frying to make it crisp; and then a final 'flavour potting' in the wok with Sichuan pepper and chilli for that signature numbing heat. The end result is a delicious snack to have on any occasion.

200 g red-braised brisket (see page 20)
vegetable oil, for deep-frying
1½ tablespoons peanut oil
2 cm knob of ginger, finely chopped
2 cloves garlic, finely chopped
2 teaspoons dark soy sauce
80 ml (⅓ cup) Chinese chicken stock (see page 17)
½ teaspoon white sugar
1 teaspoon roasted and ground Sichuan pepper (see page 17)
2 teaspoons chilli oil

sesame oil and finely sliced spring onion, to serve

TO DEEP-FRY THE BEEF

Cut the red-braised brisket into 1 cm thick slices. In a wok, heat the deep-frying oil to 180°C and deep-fry the brisket for 1 minute or until dark and crispy (like soft jerky), then drain on paper towel.

Wipe the wok clean, then place over medium heat and add the peanut oil. When the oil is hot, add the ginger and garlic and stir-fry until fragrant, then add the brisket and the rest of the ingredients. Cook until the sauce is thick and almost reduced to a glaze.

TO FINISH

Transfer to a serving plate, drizzle with sesame oil and garnish with finely sliced spring onion, then serve.

SPICE-FRIED CHICKEN WINGS WITH HEAVEN-FACING CHILLIES

Serves 4–6 as part of a shared meal

These wings are legendary at the restaurant: the initial steeping in master stock makes them super-tender, while their coating is crisp and the chilli oil is fiery hot.

3 litres master stock (see page 18)
1 kg chicken wings, jointed, wing tips discarded

TO COOK THE CHICKEN WINGS

Place the stock in a stockpot or large heavy-based saucepan and bring to the boil. Taste for seasoning and adjust accordingly. Turn off the heat, add the chicken wings to the stock and leave to steep, uncovered, until the stock is cool.

Gently lift the chicken wings out of the stock. Drain well, then chill in the fridge for 2 hours – this dries the skin of the wings, so the flour coating won't cake on them.

500 g (3⅓ cups) plain flour
75 g (¼ cup) roasted and ground
Sichuan pepper (see page 17)
1 tablespoon fine salt
vegetable oil, for deep-frying

TO DEEP-FRY THE CHICKEN WINGS

In a wide shallow bowl, mix the flour with the Sichuan pepper and the salt.

In a wok, heat the deep-frying oil to 180°C. Working in batches, coat the chicken wings in the flour and deep-fry for 3 minutes or until golden, crispy and cooked through. Drain on paper towel.

50 ml peanut oil
30 heaven-facing chillies
1 teaspoon Sichuan peppercorns
½ teaspoon chilli flakes
a lemon half

TO FINISH

Place a wok over medium heat and add the oil. When the oil is hot, add the heaven-facing chillies, Sichuan peppercorns and chilli flakes and fry until fragrant. Add the chicken wings and toss through the chilli mixture, then transfer to a platter and serve with the lemon half.

LAMB AND CUMIN PANCAKES

Serves 4–6 as part of a shared meal

Breads and pancakes like these are a familiar sight in the Xinjiang region of north-west China, where the food culture has been heavily influenced by the Muslim traders who travelled the Silk Road – and by their descendants who now call this remote part of China home. Serve these with a bowl of dark chilli paste (see page 15) to the side.

PANCAKE DOUGH

500 g (3⅓ cups) plain flour, plus extra for dusting
1 teaspoon fine salt
300 ml water

Combine the flour, salt and water in a bowl and use your hands to bring together into a dough. Transfer to a lightly floured bench and knead for 10 minutes or until smooth and elastic, then wrap in cling film and leave to rest for 30 minutes.

LAMB AND CUMIN FILLING

2 tablespoons cumin seeds, roasted
2 cm knob of ginger, roughly chopped
500 g lamb mince
2 tablespoons light soy sauce
2 teaspoons potato starch

Using a mortar and pestle, pound the cumin seeds to a coarse powder. Add the ginger and pound to a paste. Transfer to a bowl, then add the rest of the ingredients and mix well.

TO ASSEMBLE THE PANCAKES

Divide both the dough and the lamb filling into 20 even-sized portions. Roll the dough portions into balls, then roll out into rounds about 3 mm thick. Spread a portion of the filling evenly over a pancake, then cover with another pancake, pressing the edges together all around to seal well. Repeat with the remaining pancakes and filling.

TO FINISH

2 tablespoons peanut oil
sea salt

Place a heavy-based frying pan over medium–high heat, add the oil and, working in batches, pan-fry the pancakes until golden on both sides and the filling is cooked through, flipping them once. Drain on paper towel, then cut into wedges and season with sea salt before serving.

MUSSELS WITH XO SAUCE, BACON AND SPRING ONION PANCAKE

Serves 4–6 as part of a shared meal

Mussels and classic Chinese sauces like black bean and chilli are a match made in heaven, but here we take things up a notch by adding XO sauce to the mussels and serving a spring onion pancake on the side for soaking up all the salty juices – truly mouth-watering.

SPRING ONION PANCAKE

100 g (⅔ cup) plain flour, plus extra for dusting
1½ tablespoons boiling water
1½ tablespoons cold water
50 g pork lardo, chopped
1 spring onion, finely chopped
1 teaspoon sea salt
vegetable oil, for pan-frying

Place the flour in a mixing bowl and make a well in the centre. Mix the boiling water and cold water together, then add to the flour. Working from the centre outwards, use your hands to bring together into a dough. Transfer to a lightly floured bench and knead for 6 minutes, then wrap in cling film and leave to rest for 2 hours.

Roll out the dough to a thickness of about 1 cm, then scatter over the lardo, spring onion and sea salt. Use your hands to roll up the dough into a long 'snake', then coil the 'snake' into a round concentric bundle. Use a rolling pin to flatten it out into a smooth, round pancake.

Preheat the oven to 150°C. Place a heavy-based frying pan over low heat, add a film of oil and gently pan-fry the pancake for 2 minutes on each side or until golden. Drain on paper towel, then cut into wedges. Keep warm in the oven while you cook the mussels.

MUSSELS WITH XO SAUCE

500 g black mussels, debearded
100 ml Chinese chicken stock (see page 17)
25 g potato starch
100 ml water
2 teaspoons vegetable oil
10 g bacon, cut into thin strips
2 tablespoons XO sauce (see page 14)
50 ml light soy sauce
2 teaspoons white sugar

Place a heavy-based saucepan with a tight-fitting lid over medium heat. Add the mussels and stock, then cover and steam for 5 minutes or until the mussels have opened. Remove the mussels and set aside, reserving their cooking liquid.

In a small bowl, combine the potato starch with the water to make a slurry. Heat a wok over high heat, add the oil and stir-fry the bacon for a minute, then add the XO sauce and stir-fry until fragrant. Add the strained mussel-cooking liquid, along with the soy sauce, sugar and a quarter of the potato starch slurry. Stir until the sauce thickens, then add more of the slurry if needed to achieve a light sauce consistency.

TO FINISH

coriander leaves, to serve

Add the mussels to the sauce and gently reheat, then transfer to a serving bowl. Scatter with coriander and serve with the spring onion pancake.

NOODLES

STIR-FRIED SCALLOPS WITH HANDMADE WHEAT NOODLES AND CAPSICUM AND CHILLI PASTE

Serves 4–6 as part of a shared meal, or 1–2 as a one-dish meal

This noodle dish is great with any seafood. I also like it with shredded white-cut chicken (see page 18): simply fold the cooked chicken into the noodles to warm through just before serving.

NOODLES

250 g (1⅔ cups) plain flour, plus extra for dusting
135 ml water
1 teaspoon fine salt
vegetable oil

Combine all the ingredients, except the vegetable oil, in a bowl. Use your hands to bring together into a dough, then transfer to a lightly floured bench and knead for 10 minutes or until smooth. Wrap in cling film and leave to rest for 30 minutes, then repeat the kneading and resting process once more.

Roll the dough through a pasta machine to a 3 mm thickness, then place the noodle sheets on a floured board and cut into 1 cm wide noodles. Bring a saucepan of salted water to the boil, add the noodles and blanch for 2 minutes, then refresh under cold running water. Drain the noodles well and leave to dry for 5 minutes, then coat lightly with the oil to prevent them sticking.

TO COOK THE SCALLOPS

1 teaspoon peanut oil
6 scallops, roe removed

Place a wok over high heat and add the oil. When the oil is hot, briefly sear the scallops, then remove the scallops from the wok.

CAPSICUM AND CHILLI PASTE

1 teaspoon peanut oil
50 g red capsicum (pepper), cut into 1.5 cm dice
50 g green capsicum (pepper), cut into 1.5 cm dice
1 teaspoon finely chopped garlic
1 teaspoon finely chopped ginger
1 tablespoon chilli bean paste
2 teaspoons white sugar
2 teaspoons Shaoxing wine
2½ tablespoons Chinese chicken stock (see page 17)
2 teaspoons light soy sauce

Place a wok over high heat and add the oil. When the oil is hot, add the red and green capsicum, garlic and ginger and stir-fry until fragrant, then add the chilli bean paste and sugar and stir-fry for another minute. Pour in the Shaoxing wine and stock, stirring to deglaze the wok, then add the noodles and soy sauce.

TO FINISH

1 teaspoon sesame oil
1 teaspoon chilli oil
finely sliced spring onion, to serve

Stir for a moment to warm the noodles through, then finish with the sesame oil and chilli oil. Transfer to a serving bowl, place the scallops on top and garnish with spring onion.

EGG NOODLES WITH SCALLOPS AND XO SAUCE

Serves 4–6 as part of a shared meal, or 1–2 as a one-dish meal

Any seafood you like can be substituted here – I love this with prawns or crab meat.
If you're not up to making egg noodles from scratch, just use 200 g ready-made
fine egg noodles.

EGG NOODLES

250 g (1⅔ cups) plain flour, plus extra for dusting
3 egg yolks
1 large egg
½ teaspoon fine salt
vegetable oil, for coating

Combine all the ingredients, except the vegetable oil, in a bowl. Use your hands to bring together into a dough, then transfer to a lightly floured bench and knead for 10 minutes or until smooth. Wrap in cling film and leave to rest for 30 minutes.

Roll the dough through a pasta machine to a 2 mm thickness, then cut into noodles using the spaghetti attachment on the pasta machine. Bring a saucepan of salted water to the boil, add the noodles and blanch for 2 minutes, then refresh under cold running water. Drain the noodles well and leave to dry for 5 minutes, then coat lightly with the oil to prevent them sticking.

SCALLOPS AND XO SAUCE

1 teaspoon peanut oil
6 scallops, roe removed
100 g XO sauce (see page 14)
2 teaspoons white sugar
1 tablespoon light soy sauce

Place a heavy-based frying pan or wok over high heat and add the oil. When the oil is hot, sear the scallops briefly, then remove from the pan. Add the XO sauce, sugar, soy sauce and noodles to the pan and toss everything together to warm through.

TO SERVE

spring onion, cut into julienne strips

Transfer the noodle mixture to a serving bowl or platter, place the scallops on top and garnish with spring onion.

HANDMADE YELLOW NOODLES WITH BRAISED BRISKET, CHILLI AND SICHUAN PEPPER

Serves 4–6 as part of a shared meal, or 1–2 as a one-dish meal

These thick noodles are nice and chewy, and the brisket melts in your mouth.
I love all the Spice Temple noodle dishes, but this is a particular favourite.

YELLOW NOODLES

250 g (1⅔ cups) plain flour, plus extra for dusting
135 ml water
1 teaspoon fine salt
2 teaspoons turmeric powder
vegetable oil, for coating

Combine all the ingredients, except the vegetable oil, in a bowl. Use your hands to bring together into a dough, then transfer to a lightly floured bench and knead for 10 minutes or until smooth. Wrap in cling film and leave to rest for 30 minutes, then repeat the kneading and resting process once more.

Roll the dough through a pasta machine to a 3 mm thickness, then place the noodle sheets on a floured board and cut into 1.5 cm wide noodles. Bring a saucepan of salted water to the boil, add the noodles and blanch for 2 minutes, then refresh under cold running water. Drain the noodles well and leave to dry for 5 minutes, then coat lightly with the oil to prevent them sticking.

CHILLI AND SICHUAN PEPPER

1 tablespoon peanut oil
1 teaspoon Sichuan peppercorns
4 dried long red chillies
1 teaspoon finely chopped garlic
1 teaspoon finely chopped ginger
1 tablespoon chilli bean paste
1 tablespoon sweet bean paste
2 teaspoons Shaoxing wine
50 ml Chinese chicken stock (see page 17)
1 teaspoon dark soy sauce

Place a wok over high heat and add the oil. When the oil is hot, add the Sichuan peppercorns and chillies and stir-fry until fragrant. Add the garlic, ginger, chilli bean paste and sweet bean paste and stir-fry for 2 minutes. Pour in the rest of the ingredients, stirring to combine and deglaze the wok.

TO FINISH

100 g red-braised brisket (see page 20), shredded
1 teaspoon sesame oil
1 teaspoon chilli oil
finely sliced spring onion, to serve

Add the noodles and brisket to the wok and stir for a moment to warm through, then finish with the sesame oil and chilli oil and serve garnished with the spring onion.

CRISPY CHOW MEIN AUSTRALIAN–CHINESE STYLE

Serves 4–6 as part of a shared meal, or 1–2 as a one-dish meal

For this, fresh fine egg noodles from Chinatown or the supermarket work better than homemade ones. I like these crispy noodles with the Stir-fried quail and peanuts (see page 174), pipis cooked with XO sauce, or mussels and black bean sauce. Whatever you serve them with, they make for fun eating, as they soften in the sauce but still have a crunch.

vegetable oil, for deep-frying
100 g fresh fine egg noodles
25 g potato starch
100 ml water
50 ml peanut oil
120 g pork mince
2 cloves garlic, finely chopped
2 cm knob of ginger, finely chopped
30 g pickled mustard greens, finely chopped
20 g salted radish, finely chopped
1 tablespoon Tianjin preserved cabbage,
finely chopped
1 teaspoon salted chillies (see page 15)
1 tablespoon white sugar
1 tablespoon Shaoxing wine
300 ml Chinese chicken stock (see page 17)
3 teaspoons light soy sauce
3 teaspoons dark soy sauce

CRISPY CHOW MEIN

For the crispy noodles, heat the deep-frying oil to 180°C. Add the noodles and deep-fry for 1½ minutes or until crisp and golden. Drain on paper towel.

In a small bowl, combine the potato starch with the water to make a slurry.

Place a wok over high heat and add the peanut oil. When the oil is hot, add the pork mince and stir-fry until golden, then remove from the wok. In the same oil, stir-fry the garlic and ginger until fragrant, then add the mustard greens, salted radish, Tianjin preserved cabbage and salted chillies and stir-fry for a moment. Return the pork mince to the wok, then add the sugar, Shaoxing wine, stock, light and dark soy sauces and roughly half of the potato starch slurry. Stir until the sauce thickens, then add more of the slurry, as needed, stirring until you have a thick sauce.

Place the crispy noodles in a serving bowl and ladle over the sauce.

1 teaspoon sesame oil
1 teaspoon chilli oil
finely sliced spring onion, to serve

TO FINISH

Finish with the sesame oil and chilli oil and garnish with spring onion just before serving.

EGG NOODLES WITH XO AND BACON

Serves 4–6 as part of a shared meal, or 1–2 as a one-dish meal

I love the deeply savoury flavours in this noodle dish, offset by the freshness
of garlic chives and the crunch of bean sprouts. If you're short of time,
use 200 g ready-made fresh fine egg noodles instead of making your own.

EGG NOODLES

250 g (1⅔ cups) plain flour,
plus extra for dusting
3 egg yolks
1 large egg
½ teaspoon fine salt
vegetable oil, for coating

Combine all the ingredients, except the vegetable oil, in a bowl. Use your hands to
bring together into a dough, then transfer to a lightly floured bench and knead for
10 minutes or until smooth. Wrap in cling film and leave to rest for 30 minutes.

Roll the dough through a pasta machine to a 2 mm thickness, then cut into
noodles using the spaghetti attachment on the pasta machine. Bring a saucepan of
salted water to the boil, add the noodles and blanch for 2 minutes, then refresh
under cold running water. Drain the noodles well and leave to dry for 5 minutes,
then coat lightly with the oil to prevent them sticking.

XO AND BACON

1 teaspoon peanut oil
100 g bacon, cut into fine strips
100 g XO sauce (see page 14)
2 teaspoons white sugar
1 tablespoon light soy sauce
50 g bean sprouts, trimmed
50 g garlic chives, cut into 5 cm lengths

Place a heavy-based frying pan or wok over high heat and add the oil. When the
oil is hot, fry the bacon until crispy, then add the XO sauce, sugar, soy sauce,
bean sprouts, garlic chives and noodles to the pan and toss everything together to
warm through.

TO SERVE

finely shredded spring onion

Transfer the noodle mixture to a platter or serving bowl and garnish with
spring onion.

HANDMADE EGG NOODLES HUNAN-STYLE WITH SMOKED BACON AND CHILLI

Serves 4–6 as part of a shared meal, or 1–2 as a one-dish meal

This super-hot and smoky noodle dish was inspired by a Hunanese dish I once
ate, which had slivers of smoked beef stirred through it – and lots of chilli.
The result is damn tasty.

EGG NOODLES

250 g (1⅔ cups) plain flour,
plus extra for dusting

3 egg yolks

1 large egg

½ teaspoon fine salt

vegetable oil, for coating

Combine all the ingredients, except the vegetable oil, in a bowl. Use your hands
to bring together into a dough, then transfer to a lightly floured bench and knead
for 10 minutes or until smooth. Wrap in cling film and leave to rest for 30 minutes.

Roll the dough through a pasta machine to a 2 mm thickness, then cut into
noodles using the spaghetti attachment on the pasta machine. Bring a saucepan of
salted water to the boil, add the noodles and blanch for 2 minutes, then refresh
under cold running water. Drain the noodles well and leave to dry for 5 minutes,
then coat lightly with the oil to prevent them sticking.

SMOKED BACON AND CHILLI

1 teaspoon peanut oil

5 dried long red chillies

2 cm knob of ginger, finely chopped

4 cloves garlic, finely chopped

150 g smoked bacon, cut into fine strips

1½ tablespoons light soy sauce

1½ tablespoons Chinkiang black vinegar

1 teaspoon white sugar

100 g salted radish

Place a heavy-based frying pan or wok over high heat and add the oil. When the
oil is hot, add the chillies and briefly stir-fry until fragrant, then remove from
the pan or wok. In the same oil, stir-fry the ginger, garlic and bacon for a minute,
then add the rest of the ingredients and return the fried chillies to the pan or wok.

TO FINISH

crushed roasted unsalted peanuts

roasted sesame seeds

finely sliced spring onion

Add the noodles to the pan or wok and quickly toss everything together to warm
through. Transfer the noodles to a serving bowl and garnish with the peanuts,
sesame seeds and spring onion.

LUCKY DUCK NOODLES
WITH PICKLED VEGETABLES

Serves 4–6 as part of a shared meal, or 1–2 as a one-dish meal

Despite tasting incredible, this noodle dish languished on the menu at
Spice Temple ... until we called it 'lucky duck noodles'. Now it flies out of the
kitchen! Serve these with a bowl of pickled cabbage and radish (see page 24)
and sliced fresh red chillies.

100 g fresh fine egg noodles
50 ml peanut oil
100 g red-braised duck (see page 20), sliced
1 cm knob of ginger, finely chopped
2 cloves garlic, finely chopped
50 ml Shaoxing wine
1 tablespoon pickled mustard greens, chopped
1 tablespoon salted radish, chopped
1 tablespoon Tianjin preserved cabbage, chopped
2 teaspoons white sugar
1½ tablespoons light soy sauce
100 ml Chinese chicken stock (see page 17)

LUCKY DUCK NOODLES

Blanch the egg noodles in a saucepan of boiling water for 2–3 minutes, then drain
and stir through a tablespoon of the oil to prevent them sticking.

Place a wok over high heat and add a tablespoon of the peanut oil. When
the oil is hot, stir-fry the duck until golden, then remove from the wok. Add the
remaining peanut oil and stir-fry the ginger and garlic until fragrant. Pour in
the Shaoxing wine, stirring to deglaze the wok, then add the mustard greens, salted
radish, preserved cabbage, sugar and soy sauce. Return the duck to the wok, add
the stock and noodles and toss everything together to warm through. Simmer to
slightly reduce the sauce, then transfer to a serving bowl.

1 tablespoon chilli oil
2 teaspoons sesame oil
crushed roasted unsalted peanuts and finely
sliced spring onion, to serve

TO FINISH

Finish with the chill oil and sesame oil, then garnish with the peanuts and
spring onion.

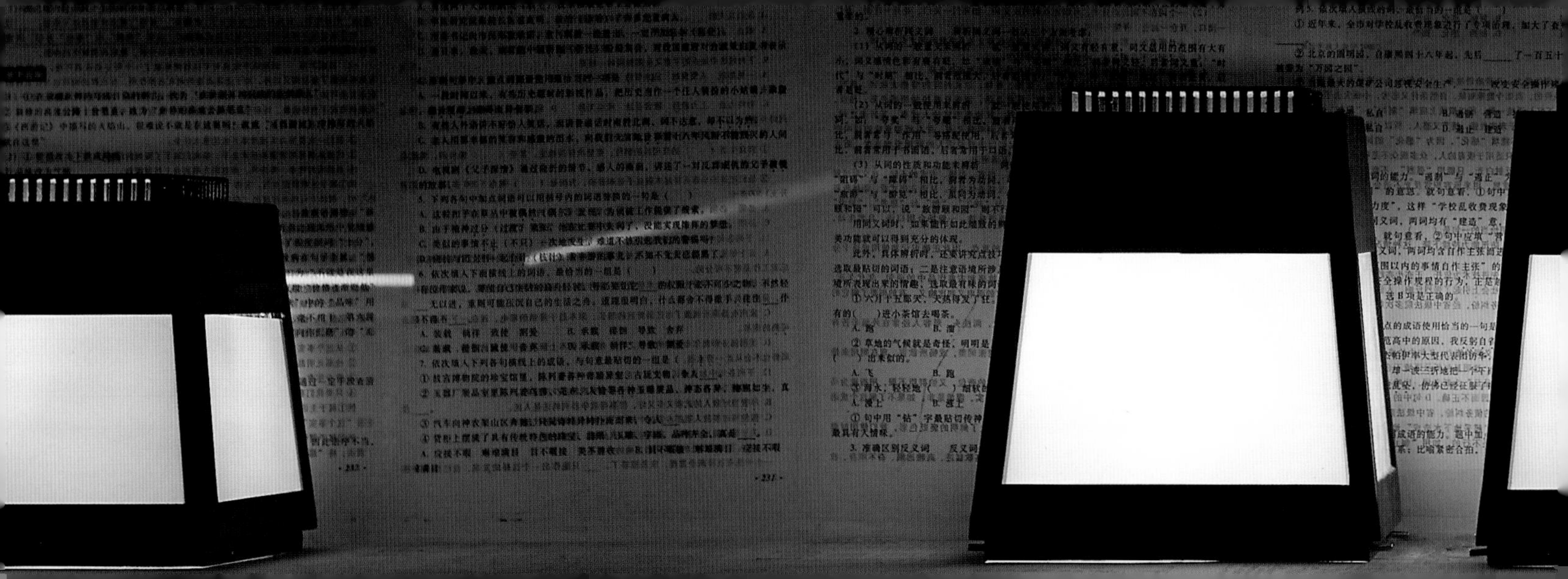

STEAMED RICE

Serves 8

I always cook this much rice for reliable results. Freeze any leftover rice
promptly and use for fried rice.

500 g (2½ cups) jasmine rice
750 ml (3 cups) cold water

Place the rice in a heavy-based saucepan with a tight-fitting lid and rinse well by running in enough cold water to cover, then pouring the water out; do this two or three times.

Add the water to the pan of rice and bring to the boil over medium–high heat. Immediately put the lid onto the pan and reduce the heat to low, then cook for 10 minutes or until the water is completely absorbed.

Turn off the heat and leave the rice to sit in the pan, still covered, for at least another 5 minutes. Serve hot or at room temperature. Fluff with a fork before serving.

FRIED RICE WITH LAP YUK, PEAS AND SALTED CHILLI >

Serves 4–6 as part of a shared meal, or 1–2 as a one-dish meal

2 eggs
½ teaspoon salted chillies (see page 15)
1 tablespoon mushroom soy sauce
50 g peas
fine salt
100 ml peanut oil
50 g lap yuk or bacon, finely sliced
400 g steamed rice (see above)
3 teaspoons sesame oil

Crack the eggs into a small bowl, then add the salted chillies and mushroom soy sauce and mix together.

Blanch the peas in a small saucepan of boiling salted water for 1 minute, then drain.

Place a wok over high heat and add the peanut oil. When the oil is hot, fry the lap yuk until fragrant, then add the egg mixture and scramble, breaking up the egg with a wok spoon. Add the rice and stir-fry for 5 minutes or until it becomes dry and fluffy.

Stir through the peas and sesame oil, then serve.

FRIED RICE WITH CONPOY

Serves 4–6 as part of a shared meal, or 1–2 as a one-dish meal

The earthy flavour of dried scallop paste, or 'conpoy',
transforms this simple fried rice.

2 eggs
50 g dried scallop (conpoy) paste
1 teaspoon salted chillies (see page 15)
1 tablespoon mushroom soy sauce
100 ml peanut oil
400 g steamed rice (see page 134)
50 g bean sprouts, trimmed
50 g garlic chives, cut into 5 cm lengths
3 teaspoons sesame oil

Crack the eggs into a small bowl, then add the conpoy, salted chillies and soy sauce and mix together.

Place a wok over high heat and add the peanut oil. When the oil is hot, add the egg mixture and scramble, breaking up the egg with a wok spoon. Add the rice and stir-fry for 5 minutes or until it becomes dry and fluffy.

Stir through the bean sprouts, garlic chives and sesame oil, then serve.

FRIED RICE YUNNAN-STYLE WITH WILD MUSHROOMS AND CHILLI

Serves 4–6 as part of a shared meal, or 1–2 as a one-dish meal

Yunan food reflects the ingredients used by and cooking styles of the majority Han Chinese, as well as the various ethnic minorities of this province. Foraging, especially for wild mushrooms, is a large part of the regional food culture. Here the mushrooms add a beautiful, earthy flavour to the rice.

2 eggs
1 fresh long red chilli, finely sliced
1 fresh long green chilli, finely sliced
1 tablespoon mushroom soy sauce
25 g dried golden mushrooms, soaked in water for 1 hour
25 g dried drumstick mushrooms, soaked in water for 1 hour
100 ml peanut oil
25 g fresh black fungi, torn into smaller pieces
25 g oyster mushrooms
25 g fresh white fungi, torn into smaller pieces
25 g fresh shiitake mushrooms, stalks removed, caps sliced
50 g lap cheong, diced
400 g steamed rice (see page 134)
50 g fried tofu cubes, for garnish
3 teaspoons sesame oil

Crack the eggs into a small bowl, then add the red and green chillies and soy sauce and mix together.

Drain the soaked mushrooms and chop roughly.

Place a wok over high heat and add 50 ml of the peanut oil. When the oil is hot, stir-fry all the dried and fresh mushrooms and fungi for 2 minutes, then remove from the wok. Add the remaining peanut oil and stir-fry the lap cheong until fragrant, then pour in the egg mixture and scramble, breaking up the egg with a wok spoon. Add the rice and stir-fry for 5 minutes or until it becomes dry and fluffy.

Return the cooked mushrooms and fungi to the wok, scatter with the fried tofu and finish with the sesame oil.

SEAFOOD

HOW TO PREPARE
LIVE CRAB AND LOBSTER

For optimum freshness, buy a live crab or lobster and dispatch it just before cooking. If you're not comfortable with doing this, you can always ask the fishmonger to do it for you, as long as you head straight home, then cook your crab or lobster immediately.

Preparing a live crab

Remove any wrapping from your crab, but leave the string around its claws. Place the crab in a freezer to put it to sleep – this may take as long as 2½ hours, depending on the size of the crab – it should no longer be moving, and shouldn't react when its mouthparts are touched.

The next bit gets messy, so wear an apron and gloves if you wish. Take the crab from the freezer and remove the string from its claws. To dispatch the crab humanely, you need to cut through its nerve centres. Place the crab on a chopping board with its head facing you. Carefully insert a sharp knife between its eyes. Turn it upside down in your sink (juice will come out, so it's definitely best to do this in the sink), then pull up the V-shaped flap at the back and carefully lift the whole top shell off. Remove the grey, feathery gills by scraping them out with a spoon or your fingers. Turn on the cold tap and thoroughly wash out the guts (usually yellow or orange) and head under running water. Snap off the V-shaped flap, chop the crab in half between the eyes with a cleaver or large chef's knife, then clean out any remaining yellow/orange internal organs. Cut each crab half in half again, cutting between the claw and the legs. Remove any excess cartilage from around the head. With a meat mallet or knife-sharpening steel, crack the claws a couple of times so the meat will be easier to extract after cooking.

Preparing a live lobster

Put your lobster into the freezer for an hour or two, to put it to sleep – it should no longer be moving, and shouldn't react when its mouthparts are touched.

To dispatch your lobster humanely, you now need to cut through its nerve centres. Put the lobster onto a chopping board with its head facing you. Carefully insert a sharp knife between its eyes. Holding the tail, cut lengthways down towards yourself, cutting quickly and firmly right through the shell. Turn the lobster around and, holding the lobster by the head, cut crossways through the tail; you should now have two halves. Pull out the digestive tract that runs down the length of the lobster.

STIR-FRIED MILK WITH CORN AND SPANNER CRAB

Serves 4–6 as part of a shared meal

Delicate egg white and milk stir-fries are a feature of Cantonese cooking – you
see them in Hong Kong all the time, usually with seafood as the main ingredient.

2 egg whites	Place the egg whites, milk and cornflour in a blender and blend until smooth.
100 ml whole milk	Place a wok over medium heat and add the vegetable oil. When the oil is hot,
1½ teaspoons cornflour	add the corn and stir-fry for 1 minute, then add the crab and cook until it is just
2 teaspoons vegetable oil	done – the crab meat should still be slightly translucent. Remove the corn and
100 g corn kernels	crab from the wok and set aside.
100 g raw spanner crab meat	Place the egg white mixture in a small heavy-based saucepan over low heat and
1 teaspoon sesame oil	warm gently, stirring constantly, until it just sets and becomes fluffy. Immediately
sea salt	remove from the heat, then stir through the corn and crab mixture and the sesame oil.
pinch of freshly ground white pepper	Season with salt and pepper, then garnish with the spring onion, transfer to
1 teaspoon finely sliced spring onion	a serving plate and serve.

PIPIS WITH BLACK OLIVE
AND BLACK BEAN DRESSING

Serves 4–6 as part of a shared meal

The salted Chinese olives used here are delicious and quite unlike anything else.
Their deep, rich, salty character works really well with the black beans and salted
radish to make a great dressing for any shellfish.

BLACK OLIVE PASTE

3 teaspoons fermented black beans
3 teaspoons finely chopped salted Chinese olives
3 teaspoons finely chopped salted radish
1 cm knob of ginger, finely chopped
1 clove garlic, finely chopped
2 tablespoons peanut oil
1½ teaspoons white vinegar
1 spring onion, finely sliced
3 teaspoons light soy sauce
2 teaspoons caster sugar

Use a pestle and mortar to lightly pound the black beans. Transfer to a bowl, add all the remaining ingredients and mix well.

TO COOK THE PIPIS

150 ml Chinese chicken stock (see page 17)
500 g pipis or clams

Pour the stock into a wok or saucepan big enough to hold the pipis. Bring to the boil, then add the pipis and simmer until they open. Remove the pipis from the wok or pan as they open and set aside, reserving the pipi-cooking stock.

TO FINISH

1 tablespoon sesame oil
1 spring onion, finely sliced

Place a wok over medium heat. Add the black olive paste, the cooked pipis and a tablespoon or two of the pipi-cooking stock and heat just until the olive paste is warmed through.

Stir in the sesame oil, then transfer to a serving bowl or plate and garnish with spring onion to serve.

BLACK BEAN AND CHILLI MUD CRAB

Serves 4–6 as part of a shared meal

Crab and black beans seem to have a particular affinity,
but this simple black bean and chilli sauce will also enhance prawns,
lobster or clams, as well as most fish.

50 g salted chillies (see page 15)
3 teaspoons fermented black beans
2 cm knob of ginger, cut into fine julienne strips
1 teaspoon caster sugar
1 teaspoon Shaoxing wine
1 teaspoon light soy sauce
1 teaspoon Chinese chicken stock (see page 17)

BLACK BEAN SAUCE
Combine all the ingredients in a small bowl and mix well.

1 × 1 kg raw mud crab, cleaned (see page 142)

MUD CRAB
Cut the mud crab body into quarters, then cut each of the large claws in two. Arrange the crab neatly on a heatproof plate that will fit in your steamer, then spoon over the black bean sauce. Place in the steamer and steam over simmering water for 6 minutes or until the crab is just cooked. To check, crack open the biggest claw – the meat should be opaque, not translucent.

100 ml peanut oil
1 spring onion, cut into fine julienne strips

TO FINISH
Heat the oil in a small heavy-based saucepan until almost smoking. Scatter the spring onion over the crab, then carefully pour over the hot oil. Serve immediately.

SALT AND PEPPER BLUE SWIMMER CRAB >

Serves 4–6 as part of a shared meal

All kinds of seafood, including squid, prawns and fish cubes or strips, can be cooked in this way – with irresistible results.

200 g (1⅓ cups) plain flour
25 g fine salt
50 g freshly ground white pepper
350 g raw blue swimmer crabs, cleaned and cut into pieces (see page 142)
vegetable oil, for deep-frying
lemon or lime wedges, to serve

In a wide shallow bowl, mix the flour with the salt and pepper. Dust the crab with the seasoned flour, letting it sit in the bowl for a minute or two so it gets a good coating.

Heat the deep-frying oil to 190°C. Working in batches, deep-fry the crab for 2 minutes or until just cooked. Drain well on paper towel.

Serve with lemon or lime wedges.

GINGER AND SPRING ONION LOBSTER

Serves 4–6 as part of a shared meal

A classic Cantonese way of cooking seafood, this method also shows off fantastically fresh white-fleshed fish, either whole or fillets. I even like to finish fried chicken with this ginger, spring onion and hot peanut oil dressing!

1 × 1 kg raw lobster, cleaned (see page 142) and cut in half
4 cm knob of ginger, cut into fine julienne strips
2 spring onions, cut into fine julienne strips
1½ tablespoons light soy sauce
1½ tablespoons Shaoxing wine
1 teaspoon caster sugar
100 ml peanut oil

Place the lobster halves, flesh side up, in a heatproof shallow bowl or lipped plate that will fit in your steamer. Scatter over the ginger and half of the spring onion, then transfer to the steamer.

In a small bowl, mix together the soy sauce, Shaoxing wine and sugar, stirring until the sugar has dissolved, then pour over the lobster. Steam the lobster over simmering water for 6 minutes or until the flesh is just cooked – the meat should be opaque, not translucent.

Meanwhile, heat the oil in a small heavy-based saucepan until almost smoking. When the lobster is cooked, scatter over the remaining spring onion and carefully pour over the hot oil. Serve immediately.

JIANGXI-STYLE
STEAMED FLATHEAD

Serves 4 as part of a shared meal

I'll never forget my first taste of this, at a Jiangxi restaurant in Beijing. We had a few dishes that impressed that day, but this has become one of my favourite fish dishes of all time – the flavours and textures are perfect. If flathead is not available, you could use another white fish such as cod instead.

DRESSING

100 ml peanut oil
2 tablespoons sesame oil
40 g caster sugar
50 ml light soy sauce

Mix all the ingredients together in a small bowl, stirring until the sugar has dissolved.

STEAMED FLATHEAD

250 g flathead fillets, skin off
20 g pickled mustard greens, finely chopped
10 g salted radish, finely chopped
20 g salted chillies (see page 15)
20 g pickled green chillies (see page 15), finely chopped

Place the fish fillets in a single layer in a heatproof shallow bowl or lipped plate that will fit in your steamer. Scatter with the rest of the ingredients, then transfer to the steamer. Pour over the dressing and steam the fish over boiling water for 7 minutes or until it is just cooked.

TO SERVE

½ spring onion, finely sliced
¼ teaspoon roasted sesame seeds

Place the fish fillets in a serving bowl and pour over all the cooking juices, then garnish with the spring onion and sesame seeds.

HUNAN-STYLE STEAMED BLUE-EYE TREVALLA WITH SALTED RED CHILLI AND PICKLED GREEN CHILLI

Serves 4–6 as part of a shared meal

Rustic and full of flavour, food from Hunan is often even hotter than that of its neighbouring province, Sichuan, but its heat tends to come from fresh rather than dried chillies. Here, red and green chillies are salted and pickled respectively, giving the fish a striking appearance and a fiery, complex flavour.

1 × 250 g blue-eye trevalla fillet, skin off
40 g pickled green chillies (see page 15), chopped finely, plus 2 teaspoons of their pickling liquid
30 g salted chillies (see page 15)
1 teaspoon light soy sauce
2 teaspoons sesame oil

Place the fish on a heatproof plate that will fit in your steamer, then spread a layer of pickled green chillies over one half of the fish and a layer of salted chillies over the other half and place in the steamer. Drizzle the fish with the soy sauce and steam over boiling water for 7 minutes or until it is just cooked.

Carefully, lift the fish from the steamer and place in a serving bowl. Stir the sesame oil into the cooking juices on the plate in the steamer, then pour it around the fish, taking care not to disturb the green and red chilli coating. Serve immediately.

FLATHEAD DROWNED IN HEAVEN-FACING CHILLIES AND SICHUAN PEPPERCORNS

Serves 4–6 as part of a shared meal

In this classic Sichuanese dish, the fish sits in a broth beneath a layer of oil infused with chillies and Sichuan peppercorns: as you serve the fish at the table, it gets coated in the flavoured oil (the chillies and peppercorns aren't meant to be eaten!).

We loved this from the moment we first tried it at a Sichuanese restaurant in Shanghai. With this much oil, you might think the fish would be overpowered, but the Sichuan peppercorns and chilli cut through the richness to the extent that the fish tastes clean and hot. And the more you eat, the more addictive the tingling, numbing sensation becomes – a very special dish indeed.

250 g flathead fillets, skin off
3 teaspoons potato starch
2 teaspoons cold water
1 teaspoon Shaoxing wine
1 teaspoon peanut oil

TO MARINATE THE FLATHEAD
Cut the fish fillets into 1 cm thick slices. Combine the rest of the ingredients in a small bowl and mix until smooth. Add the fish, mix well with your hands and set aside for 5 minutes.

70 ml peanut oil
3 stalks celery, cut into strips about 5 cm × 1 cm
4 spring onions, cut into 5 cm lengths
100 g bean sprouts, trimmed
sea salt
625 ml (2½ cups) Chinese chicken stock
(see page 17)

TO COOK THE VEGETABLES AND FLATHEAD
Place a wok over high heat. When it is smoking hot, drizzle in the oil and stir-fry the celery, spring onion and bean sprouts with a pinch of salt for 2 minutes. Remove from the wok and place in a large serving bowl.

Wipe out the wok and return to the heat. Pour in the stock, add another pinch of salt and bring to the boil. Gently add the fish to the wok, then immediately remove from the heat and leave the fish to cook in the hot stock for 2 minutes. Transfer the fish and stock to the serving bowl with the vegetables.

20 dried small chillies, cut in half lengthways
40 heaven-facing chillies, cut in half lengthways
500 ml (2 cups) peanut oil
50 g Sichuan peppercorns

TO FINISH
Wipe out the wok and place over low heat. Add all the dried chillies to the wok and dry-roast, stirring occasionally, for 15 minutes or until fragrant. In a heavy-based saucepan, heat the oil over high heat until almost smoking. Scatter the Sichuan peppercorns and the dry-roasted chillies over the fish, then very carefully pour over the hot oil. Serve immediately.

WHOLE STEAMED SNAPPER WITH BLACK BEAN AND SALTED CHILLI

Serves 4–6 as part of a shared meal

Wonderfully aromatic, the flavour of this Sichuan-style steamed fish is amped up by being cooked with a paste of fermented beans and chilli, followed by a dousing with sizzling oil.

1 × 450–500 g snapper, cleaned and scaled
3 tablespoons salted chillies (see page 15)
1½ tablespoons fermented black beans
2 teaspoons white sugar
3 teaspoons Shaoxing wine
2 cm knob of ginger, cut into fine julienne strips
50 ml peanut oil
1 spring onion, cut into fine julienne strips

Place the snapper on a heatproof lipped plate that will fit in your steamer. In a small bowl, combine the salted chillies, black beans, sugar, Shaoxing wine and ginger, then spread over the snapper. Transfer the snapper to the steamer.

Steam the fish over boiling water for 8–10 minutes or until it is just cooked through. Carefully lift out the fish and place on a serving plate, then pour over the cooking juices. Heat the oil in a small heavy-based saucepan over high heat until almost smoking. Scatter the spring onion over the fish, then spoon the hot oil over the top and serve immediately.

HOT AND FRAGRANT PRAWNS

Serves 4–6 as part of a shared meal

This spicy and aromatic stir-fry should be quite dry, with just a little sauce clinging to the prawns. I love the versatility and complex flavour of Pixian chilli bean paste, which can be used in all kinds of stir-fries – just remember it is very salty, so tread carefully with any other salty seasoning.

50 ml peanut oil
200 g peeled and deveined raw prawns
20 g Pixian chilli bean paste
1.5 cm knob of ginger, finely chopped
100 g garlic stems, cut into 4 cm lengths
2 teaspoons white sugar
100 ml Chinese chicken stock (see page 17)
2 spring onions, cut into 4 cm lengths
1 tablespoon chilli oil
2 teaspoons sesame oil

Place a wok over high heat. When it is smoking hot, drizzle in half of the peanut oil and quickly stir-fry the prawns just until they change colour. Remove the prawns and set aside.

Reduce the heat to medium. Add the remaining peanut oil to the wok and stir-fry the chilli bean paste and ginger until fragrant. Add the garlic stems and sugar, then pour in the stock. Turn the heat back up to high and add the spring onion.

When the sauce has reduced by about half, add the rest of the ingredients. Return the cooked prawns to the wok, briefly toss everything together, then transfer to a serving plate and serve immediately.

STIR-FRIED PRAWNS WITH
SALTED DUCK EGG AND FOUR CHILLIES

Serves 4–6 as part of a shared meal

Time for some artistic licence! We sort of made up this dish while we were
testing recipes for the restaurant, so this one is a bit of a Spice Temple original.
The different kinds of chillies make it hot and complex, and the salted duck egg
yolks produce a rich, creamy sauce that's almost like a Chinese carbonara.

1 tablespoon peanut oil

200 g peeled and deveined raw prawns

2 small cloves garlic, finely chopped

1.5 cm knob of ginger, finely chopped

½ spring onion, finely sliced

½ small red onion, finely sliced

1 teaspoon chilli flakes

2 tablespoons fermented red chillies
(see page 15)

2 tablespoons salted chillies (see page 15)

2 tablespoons pickled green chillies
(see page 15)

2 teaspoons Chinese chicken stock
(see page 17)

50 ml Shaoxing wine

1 teaspoon light soy sauce

2 teaspoons white sugar

2 salted duck egg yolks, mashed

Place a wok over high heat. When it is moking hot, add a drizzle of the oil and
stir-fry the prawns with the garlic, ginger and spring onion just until the prawns
change colour. Remove all the ingredients and set aside.

Add another drizzle of oil to the wok, then add the red onion, chilli flakes,
fermented chillies, salted chillies, pickled green chillies, stock, Shaoxing wine, soy
sauce and sugar. Cook for a minute or until a sauce has formed, then return the
prawns, ginger and spring onion to the wok. Add the salted egg yolks and cook
until the sauce thickens, then immediately remove from the heat and transfer to
a serving plate.

1 tablespoon finely sliced coriander

½ teaspoon roasted and ground Sichuan
pepper (see page 17)

TO SERVE

Garnish with the coriander and Sichuan pepper and serve.

STIR-FRIED SPANNER CRAB WITH LEEK, SALTED CHILLI AND YELLOW BEANS

Serves 4–6 as part of a shared meal

This clean-tasting dish is all about the crab, with the yellow beans and salted chillies just a background hum.

60 ml (¼ cup) peanut oil
200 g raw spanner crab meat
2 cm knob of ginger, finely chopped
2 cloves garlic, finely chopped
1 tablespoon salted yellow beans, rinsed
1 tablespoon salted chillies (see page 15)
1 small leek, cut into 2 cm lengths
on the diagonal
1½ tablespoons Shaoxing wine
1 tablespoon Chinese chicken stock
(see page 17)
1 tablespoon light soy sauce
1 teaspoon freshly ground white pepper
50 g garlic chives, cut into 5 cm lengths
2 teaspoons sesame oil

Place a wok over high heat. When it is smoking hot, drizzle in half the peanut oil and quickly stir-fry the crab meat until it is just cooked. Remove the crab and set aside.

Add the remaining peanut oil to the wok and stir-fry the ginger and garlic until fragrant. Add the salted yellow beans, salted chillies and leek and cook for 20 seconds. Pour in the Shaoxing wine, stirring to deglaze the wok, then add the stock, soy sauce and pepper.

Return the cooked crab meat to the wok, add the remaining ingredients, then spoon onto a serving plate and serve immediately.

DEEP-FRIED WHOLE SNAPPER
WITH SICHUAN PEPPER AND SALT

Serves 4–6 as part of a shared meal

Any seafood can be cooked like this, to give it a tasty crust and a meltingly
tender interior.

1 × 600 g snapper, cleaned and scaled
200 g (1⅓ cups) plain flour
50 g roasted and ground Sichuan pepper
(see page 17)
25 g fine salt
vegetable oil, for deep-frying
Sichuan pepper and salt (see page 17)
2 spring onions, finely sliced
lemon wedges, to serve

Place the fish on a chopping board. With a sharp knife, deeply score the fish every
3 cm from head to tail on both sides, cutting almost to the bone.

In a wide shallow bowl, mix the flour with the Sichuan pepper and the salt.

Heat the deep-frying oil to 180°C. Dust the fish in the seasoned flour to coat,
then carefully lower it into the hot oil and deep-fry for 10 minutes or until crisp
and cooked through. Drain on paper towel.

Place the fish on a serving plate and sprinkle with Sichuan pepper and salt.
Just before serving, scatter with spring onion, then serve with wedges of lemon.

POULTRY

THREE-SHOT CHICKEN: BEER, CHILLI AND SOY

Serves 4–6 as part of a shared meal

With a shot each of beer, chilli and soy added as a final flourish, this dish brings
an element of fun to a meal. If you have a claypot and a portable stove, add
the three shots and finish the cooking at the table for a bit of theatre: pour the
contents of the wok into your claypot and place it over the portable stove,
then tip in the three shots and cook for 3 minutes before serving.

5 small dried shiitake mushrooms, soaked in
water overnight, drained
8 cloves garlic, peeled
2 tablespoons peanut oil
250 g chicken thigh fillets, cut into 2 cm chunks
1 small carrot, thinly sliced on the diagonal
3 cm knob of ginger, cut into fine julienne strips
1½ tablespoons Shaoxing wine
3 tablespoons sweet bean paste
2 tablespoons Chinese chicken stock
(see page 17)
50 ml beer
50 ml chilli oil
50 ml light soy sauce

Place the drained shiitakes in a small saucepan of water and simmer for 2 hours or
until soft.

Place the garlic cloves in another saucepan of cold water and bring to the boil,
then drain. Repeat this blanching process twice more.

Place a wok over high heat. When it is smoking hot, drizzle in half of the
peanut oil. Working in two batches, stir-fry the chicken until golden and just
cooked through, then remove and set aside in a bowl. Add the garlic cloves to the
same oil in the wok and stir-fry until fragrant. Add the carrot and drained mushrooms
and stir-fry for 30 seconds, then transfer to the bowl with the chicken.

Add the remaining oil to the wok and stir-fry the ginger until fragrant. Pour
in the Shaoxing wine, stirring to deglaze the wok, then add the bean paste and
stock and bring to the boil. Return the chicken, garlic, carrot and mushrooms to
the wok and combine with the sauce. Add the three shots and cook for 3 minutes,
then serve.

KUNG PAO CHICKEN WITH SICHUAN PEPPERCORNS, HEAVEN-FACING CHILLIES AND CASHEWS

Serves 4–6 as part of a shared meal

The story goes that this Sichuanese dish was named after a governor of Sichuan province who held office during the Qing Dynasty: his formal title was Kung Pao ('guardian of the palace'), and apparently this was one of his favourite dishes. Our version has cashew nuts where others have peanuts, but either work. Cubes of chicken are cooked with an abundance of dried chillies and Sichuan peppercorns – at the table, chopsticks are used to pick out the chicken, spring onions and nuts from the mountain of chillies and peppercorns, which will have seasoned the oil but aren't meant to be eaten.

250 g chicken thigh fillets, cut into 2 cm chunks
plain flour, for dusting
125 ml (½ cup) vegetable oil
15 dried long red chillies
10 heaven-facing chillies
1.5 cm knob of ginger, finely chopped
2 small cloves garlic, finely chopped
2 teaspoons Sichuan peppercorns
1 spring onion, cut into 5 cm lengths
1 tablespoon Shaoxing wine
1½ tablespoons light soy sauce
150 ml Chinese chicken stock (see page 17)
2 teaspoons white sugar

2 teaspoons sesame oil
30 g roasted unsalted cashews

Dust the chicken pieces with the flour. Heat 100 ml of the vegetable oil in a wok over medium heat and shallow-fry the chicken until golden and cooked through. Drain on paper towel.

Wipe out the wok, place over low–medium heat and drizzle in the remaining oil. Gently fry all of the chillies until fragrant, then remove from the wok and set aside. Add the ginger and garlic to the wok and stir-fry until fragrant, then add the Sichuan peppercorns and spring onion, together with the reserved chicken and chillies. Pour in the Shaoxing wine, stirring to deglaze the wok, then add the rest of the ingredients and stir gently until the chicken is hot and well coated in the sauce.

TO FINISH
Transfer to a serving plate, then finish with the sesame oil and roasted cashews and serve.

STIR-FRIED QUAIL AND PEANUTS WITH STEAMED EGG CUSTARD

Serves 4–6 as part of a shared meal

I love the versatility of this dish. Essentially the stir-fried quail is a meaty relish spooned on top of a savoury custard, so you can substitute rabbit, chicken, pork or beef for the quail – all go well with the chilli, peanuts and creamy custard. Depending on the texture you're after, you can chop the meat by hand or mince it (or get your butcher to mince it for you).

3 eggs
90 ml Chinese chicken stock (see page 17)

EGG CUSTARD
Whisk the eggs with the stock in a bowl, then pour into a shallow heatproof bowl that will fit in your steamer, such as a rice bowl. Cover with cling film, transfer to the steamer and steam gently over simmering water for 12–15 minutes or until the egg is just set – it should still be slightly wobbly.

60 ml (¼ cup) peanut oil
150 g minced quail
2 tablespoons Tianjin preserved cabbage, rinsed and chopped
3 tablespoons pickled mustard greens, finely chopped
1 tablespoon salted radish, finely chopped
1.5 cm knob of ginger, finely chopped
2 small cloves garlic, finely chopped
1 teaspoon light soy sauce
1 teaspoon dark soy sauce
1 teaspoon white sugar
2 teaspoons fermented red chillies (see page 15)
1 teaspoon salted chillies (see page 15)

STIR-FRIED QUAIL
Meanwhile, place a wok over high heat. When it is smoking hot, drizzle in half of the peanut oil and quickly stir-fry the quail mince until it is just cooked. Remove and set aside. Add the remaining oil, along with the preserved cabbage, pickled mustard greens, salted radish, ginger and garlic to the wok and stir-fry until fragrant, then add the rest of the ingredients. Return the quail to the wok and stir-fry until hot and well coated.

finely sliced spring onion and roasted unsalted peanuts

TO FINISH
Serve the steamed custard topped with the stir-fried quail mixture and garnished with sliced spring onion and roasted peanuts.

TEA-SMOKED DUCK WITH MANDARIN PANCAKES

Serves 8 as part of a shared meal

Prepared in this way, a whole duck will serve eight people. If you're cooking for a smaller gathering, just serve half the duck; the other half will keep for two days in the fridge and can be added to salads and stir-fries. This recipe makes about 32 pancakes: you only need 16 to serve eight people (or eight, if you're only serving half a duck for four people), but the rest can be frozen for up to three months. If you don't have time to make the mandarin pancakes, you should be able to find them ready-made in Chinese supermarkets – just steam them for a minute or two to soften and warm through.

TEA-SMOKED DUCK

1 × 2 kg duck, wing tips and parson's nose removed
20 cm knob of ginger, sliced
handful of spring onion tops
2 teaspoons Sichuan peppercorns
600 g tea-smoking mixture (see page 21)

Stuff the cavity of the duck with the ginger and spring onion tops, then scatter the Sichuan peppercorns over the skin. Place the duck in the fridge overnight. The next day, discard the ginger and spring onion and wipe off the Sichuan peppercorns.

Make a shallow bowl from foil and place it in the base of a large wok, then place the tea-smoking mixture inside. Set a wire rack over the top to hold the duck about 5 cm above the smoking mixture (if necessary, use some foil balls to elevate the rack) and cover tightly with a lid. Heat the smoking mixture in the wok over high heat until it starts to smoke, then briefly lift the lid off the wok and place the duck on the rack. Replace the lid and smoke the duck over high heat for 20 minutes.

Transfer the duck to a heatproof shallow bowl or lipped plate that will fit in your steamer and steam over rapidly simmering water for 1 hour or until cooked through, topping up the water level as needed. Carefully lift the duck from the steamer, leave to cool slightly, then refrigerate for at least 3 hours.

MANDARIN PANCAKES

400 g (2⅔ cups) plain flour, plus extra for dusting
200 ml boiling water
sesame oil, for brushing

Sift the flour into a bowl and pour in the boiling water. Mix with a wooden spoon until a dough forms, then tip out onto a floured bench and knead for 5 minutes or until smooth. Cover with a bowl and leave to rest for 1 hour. Divide the rested dough into walnut-sized balls and re-cover with the bowl.

Take two dough balls and brush the tops with sesame oil, then lay one ball on top of the other, so that the oiled sides are together. Roll out the balls to form a round about 15 cm in diameter. Continue with the remainder of the dough balls, keeping the prepared pancakes covered with a damp tea towel to prevent them from drying out.

Heat a dry heavy-based frying pan over low heat. Add one of the pancake pairs and cook until it puffs up and can be pulled apart to form two thin pancakes. Continue with the remaining pancake pairs.

HOISIN DIPPING SAUCE

200 g hoisin sauce
1 tablespoon sweet bean paste
1 tablespoon sesame oil
1 tablespoon rice wine vinegar

Place all the ingredients in a small bowl and mix together well.

TO DEEP-FRY THE DUCK

vegetable oil, for deep-frying

Using a cleaver, cut the duck in half lengthways. Heat the deep-frying oil to 180°C and deep-fry each duck half for 5 minutes or until crisp. Drain on paper towel.

TO SERVE

1 Lebanese (small) cucumber, cut into strips about 6 cm × 1 cm
4 spring onions, cut into 6 cm lengths

Stack 16 mandarin pancakes in a bamboo steamer and steam over boiling water for a couple of minutes to reheat. Carve thin slices of duck meat and skin and arrange on a platter. Serve the pancakes, dipping sauce and cucumber and spring onion alongside. Let people help themselves to pancakes, then spread them with the dipping sauce, followed by adding a piece each of cucumber and spring onion and a slice or two of duck, before rolling up and eating.

CRISP-SKINNED CHICKEN
WITH TWO DRESSINGS

Serves 4–6 as part of a shared meal

Either – or both – of these dressings work beautifully with the
tender meat and crispy fried skin of this chicken.

1 × 1.6 kg chicken, wing tips and
parson's nose removed
3 litres master stock (see page 18)

TO COOK THE CHICKEN

Remove any excess fat from the cavity of the chicken and wipe the cavity clean,
then truss. Bring a stockpot or large saucepan of water to the boil, plunge the
chicken into it and leave for 1 minute, then remove and rinse under cold running
water. Pat the chicken dry with paper towel.

Pour the master stock into a stockpot or large heavy-based saucepan and bring
to the boil. Lower the chicken into the stock, then turn off the heat and leave to
cool to room temperature before refrigerating for 24 hours. Make sure the chicken
is completely submerged in the stock – weight it down with a plate, if necessary.

Lift the chicken from the stock and place on a heatproof plate in a large steamer.
Steam the chicken over simmering water for 20–25 minutes or until cooked
through. Remove and leave to cool slightly, then chill in the fridge for at least
3 hours – this dries out the skin, so it will become crisp when deep-fried.

4 cloves garlic, finely chopped
6 cm knob of ginger, finely chopped
2 spring onions, finely sliced
2 tablespoons peanut oil
2 teaspoons lemon juice
sea salt and freshly ground white pepper

GINGER AND SPRING ONION DRESSING

Place the garlic, ginger and spring onion in a heatproof bowl. Heat the oil in a small
heavy-based saucepan over high heat until almost smoking, then carefully pour
over the garlic, ginger and spring onion. Stir through the lemon juice and season
with salt and pepper, then transfer to a small serving bowl.

50 ml water
50 g caster sugar
100 ml Chinkiang black vinegar
50 ml light soy sauce

BLACK VINEGAR DRESSING

Place the water and sugar in a small heavy-based saucepan over low heat and warm
gently, stirring to dissolve the sugar. When the sugar has dissolved, remove from the
heat and stir through the rest of the ingredients. Transfer to a small serving bowl.

vegetable oil, for deep-frying

TO DEEP-FRY THE CHICKEN

Using a cleaver or large sharp knife, cut the chicken in half lengthways. Heat the
deep-frying oil to 180°C and deep-fry each chicken half for 5 minutes or until
crisp and golden. Drain on paper towel, then chop the chicken (see page 18) and
serve with the two dressings on the side.

CRISPY SICHUAN DUCK

Serves 8 as part of a shared meal

This is a slightly easier, but equally impressive, version of Peking duck. Don't
think of these double- and triple-cooked dishes as complicated; think of them as
three simple steps, and you will find them less daunting to master.

The lengthy steaming renders the layer of fat that lies under the skin of the duck,
so it crisps up nicely when you fry it.

1 × 2 kg duck
3 teaspoons fine salt
1 teaspoon five-spice powder

TO MARINATE THE DUCK

Rinse the duck well, inside and out, then pat dry with paper towel. Remove any
excess fat from the cavity. Place the duck on a chopping board and cut off the wing
tips at the first joint. Using the palms of your hands, push down firmly on the
breastbone to snap the bones and flatten the duck slightly. Mix the salt with
the five-spice powder, then rub the mixture all over the duck, inside and out.
Cover and refrigerate overnight.

8 cm knob of ginger, cut into 4 slices
2 spring onions, cut into 4 cm lengths
2 tablespoons light soy sauce
plain flour, for dusting
vegetable oil, for deep-frying

TO COOK THE DUCK

The next day, stuff the ginger and spring onion into the duck's cavity. Place the
duck in a wide shallow heatproof bowl that will fit in your steamer and steam over
rapidly boiling water for 3 hours, topping up the water as needed. Carefully remove
the duck from the steamer, drain any liquid from its cavity, then remove the ginger
and spring onion and leave the duck to cool.

Heat the deep-frying oil to 180°C. Brush the duck all over with the soy sauce
and dust lightly with flour, blowing off any excess. Carefully lower the duck into
the hot oil and deep-fry, turning occasionally, for 12 minutes or until the skin is
crisp and golden all over. Drain on paper towel.

16 mandarin pancakes (see page 176)
4 spring onions, cut into 6 cm lengths
1 Lebanese (small) cucumber, cut into strips
about 6 cm × 1 cm
125 g hoisin sauce
2 tablespoons sesame oil

TO SERVE

Stack the mandarin pancakes in a bamboo steamer and steam over boiling water
for a couple of minutes to reheat, then fold each one into quarters. Shred the warm
duck meat and crispy skin with two forks, and arrange on a serving plate. Place the
spring onion and cucumber on a separate plate. Mix the hoisin sauce with
the sesame oil in a small bowl. Place the pancakes on another plate, and let people
fill their own pancakes at the table.

SHANGHAI-STYLE SALTWATER DUCK

Serves 8 as part of a shared meal

Although this Shanghainese duck may look almost raw, it is actually cured with
salt (just like ham), resulting in tender, tasty meat. Making it couldn't be easier:
all you need is a large stockpot – and some patience, as the duck is steeped in
brine overnight.

BRINE

600 g fine salt
6 star anise
2 teaspoons Sichuan peppercorns
1 tablespoon Shaoxing wine
2 spring onions, cut into 4 cm lengths
8 cm knob of ginger, sliced
7 litres water

Place a 10 litre-capacity stockpot on the stovetop and add all the ingredients.
Bring to the boil, then reduce the heat and simmer for 40 minutes.

SALTWATER DUCK

1 × 2 kg duck, wing tips and parson's
nose removed

Rinse the duck well, inside and out, then pat dry with paper towel. Remove any
excess fat from the cavity and prick the skin all over with a fork. Add the duck
to the brine and simmer for 15 minutes, then turn off the heat and leave the
duck to cool in the brine – you may need to weight the duck down with a plate
to keep it submerged. When cooled to room temperature, transfer to the fridge
and chill for 24 hours.

TO SERVE

chilli sauce (see page 14) and hoisin sauce

Lift the duck from the brine and chop it (see page 18) or slice it, then serve cold
with chilli sauce and hoisin sauce.

CHINESE ROAST DUCK

Serves 6–8 as part of a shared meal

This one is for when you are ready to tackle the classic Cantonese-style roast
duck, with its lacquered skin and rich meat. Treat this as a sequence of small
recipes, and you'll soon be on your way to making one of the most spectacular
duck dishes ever.

1 × 2 kg Pekin duck, with neck attached
1 teaspoon Sichuan pepper and salt
(see page 17)
3 star anise
2 cinnamon sticks

TO PREPARE AND SEASON THE DUCK

Remove any excess fat from the cavity of the duck. Place the duck on a chopping
board, breast-side up and, with the legs facing you, massage the skin on the breasts
and legs for 5 minutes – this helps to loosen the connective tissue between the
skin and the meat. Cut a small slit in the skin at the neck end and carefully work
a piece of dowel or narrow spatula down the breast and over the legs to loosen the
skin without tearing it. Once the skin is loose, rub the Sichuan pepper and salt
into the meat (under the skin), then ease the star anise and cinnamon sticks in
between the meat and skin as well, distributing them evenly.

Secure the rear cavity of the duck with a bamboo or metal skewer, weaving it
in and out as if you were sewing cloth together. Tie a double length of kitchen
string firmly around the top of the neck, above the slit, leaving one end long. Tie
off the neck below the slit using a slip knot and insert a drinking straw or the clean
tube of a bicycle pump into the slit. Inflate the cavity you have made between the
skin and the meat of the duck and, when fully inflated, tighten the slip knot around
the duck's neck to make it airtight.

200 g maltose
125 ml (½ cup) light soy sauce
60 ml (¼ cup) rice wine vinegar
5 litres water

TO GLAZE THE DUCK

Place the maltose, soy sauce, rice vinegar and water in a stockpot or large heavy-
based saucepan, then bring to the boil and cook for 5 minutes. Holding onto the
long end of the top string, immerse the duck, breast-side down, for 20 seconds. Pull
the duck up again and, holding it over the pan, baste the duck with the maltose
mixture for 5 minutes or until the skin tightens. Take care not to let the simmering
maltose mixture become too dark while you're doing this, or the glaze on the duck
will burn in the oven before the meat is cooked. Drain the excess maltose from the
duck and hang the duck to dry over a bowl in front of a fan for 3 hours. The duck
skin should now feel like parchment.

180 ml (¾ cup) Chinese chicken stock
(see page 17)
60 ml (¼ cup) light soy sauce
50 g yellow rock sugar, crushed
1 tablespoon sesame oil

TO ROAST THE DUCK

Preheat the oven to 220°C and place a roasting tin full of water on the bottom of
the oven. Place all the ingredients in a small heavy-based saucepan and bring to the
boil. Loosen the skewer from the duck's cavity just enough to insert a funnel.
Carefully pour the hot stock mixture into the cavity, then firmly secure the skewer
again. Place the duck in the oven, placing it directly onto the rungs of a shelf over
the tin of water, with its legs pointing towards the door, and roast for 45–60 minutes,
or until the juices run clear when a small sharp knife is inserted into the thickest part
of a thigh. Remove and leave to rest for 10 minutes, then remove the skewer from
the cavity and carefully strain the juices into a bowl or jug.

TO SERVE

Chop the duck (see page 18) and pour the reserved juices over the top.

MA PO OF SHREDDED DUCK, SILKEN TOFU, CHESTNUTS AND PICKLED VEGETABLES

Serves 4–6 as part of a shared meal

This is a variation on the classic Sichuanese dish of ma po tofu (or pock-marked grandmother's bean curd), which is usually made with beef or pork. For me, the substitution of duck is a wild success, with the chestnuts and pickled vegetables adding extra texture and flavour.

30 g dried chestnuts, soaked in water overnight

50 ml peanut oil

½ red-braised duck (see page 20), sliced

4 cloves garlic, finely chopped

4 cm knob of ginger, finely chopped

50 g chilli bean paste

3 teaspoons white sugar

3 teaspoons Shaoxing wine

125 ml (½ cup) Chinese chicken stock (see page 17)

1 tablespoon light soy sauce

2 tablespoons pickled mustard greens, finely chopped

1 tablespoon salted radish, finely chopped

1 tablespoon Tianjin preserved cabbage, finely chopped

1 teaspoon roasted and ground Sichuan pepper (see page 17)

1 × 300 g block silken tofu

1 spring onion, cut into 4 cm lengths

1 tablespoon chilli oil

1 tablespoon sesame oil

1 teaspoon roasted and ground Sichuan pepper (see page 17)

Drain the soaked chestnuts and place in a small saucepan of cold water. Bring to the boil and cook for 30 minutes or until tender. Drain and set aside.

Place a wok over high heat. When it is hot, drizzle in the peanut oil and briefly stir-fry the duck just to lightly colour. Remove and set aside. Add the garlic and ginger and stir-fry until fragrant, then add the chilli bean paste, sugar, Shaoxing wine, stock and soy sauce, stirring to deglaze the wok. Cook for 2 minutes or until reduced to a sauce consistency, then stir in the reserved chestnuts and duck, along with the mustard greens, salted radish, preserved cabbage and the Sichuan pepper. Cook for another minute or two, just to warm everything through.

Cut the tofu in half crossways, then into 8 pieces. Place on a heatproof plate that will fit in your steamer. Transfer to the steamer and steam the tofu over simmering water for 8 minutes.

TO FINISH

Carefully transfer the tofu to a serving bowl, then spoon over the duck and sauce. Garnish with the spring onion, drizzle over the chilli oil and sesame oil, and sprinkle with the Sichuan pepper.

HOT AND NUMBING CRISPY DUCK

Serves 4–6 as part of a shared meal

This recipe came about when we were keen to develop a spicy duck dish to contrast with the classic Chinese duck dishes on the menu. Although the sauce is a bit of a made-up one, consisting of all things spicy and numbing caramelised with sugar, this duck is one of our very best sellers. The sweet and hot sauce goes well with any fried food.

½ red-braised duck (see page 20)

2 egg whites

pinch of fine salt

30 g cornflour

vegetable oil, for deep-frying

50 ml peanut oil

4 cloves garlic, finely chopped

4 cm knob of ginger, finely chopped

3 tablespoons roasted and ground Sichuan pepper (see page 17)

3 tablespoons chilli flakes

70 g white sugar

100 ml Chinkiang black vinegar

70 ml light soy sauce

50 ml Chinese chicken stock (see page 17)

1 tablespoon chilli oil

½ spring onion, finely sliced on the diagonal

Place the duck on a heatproof lipped plate that will fit in your steamer. Whisk the egg whites with the salt until soft peaks form, then spoon over the duck. Sift the cornflour on top of the duck, then transfer to the steamer and steam over boiling water for 15 minutes. Remove and leave to cool slightly, then chill in the fridge for at least 3 hours – this dries out the skin, so it becomes crisp when deep-fried.

Heat the deep-frying oil to 180°C. Deep-fry the duck for 5 minutes or until crisp, then drain on paper towel.

Place a wok over high heat. When it is hot, drizzle in the peanut oil and stir-fry the garlic and ginger until fragrant. Add half of the Sichuan pepper, along with the chilli flakes, sugar, vinegar, soy sauce and stock. Stir to deglaze the wok, then cook for 3 minutes or until reduced to a sauce consistency. Add the chilli oil and set aside.

Cut the duck into generous slices, then arrange on a serving plate, spoon over the sauce and garnish with the spring onion and remaining Sichuan pepper.

PORK

CHINESE-STYLE BBQ PORK

Serves 6–8 as part of a shared meal

This pork can be served warm with rice, sliced as a cold cut, or added to stir-fries and soups. One of my favourite ways to start a dinner party, if indeed I'm going to serve something first, is with a plate of this pork, white-cut chicken (see page 18) and tea eggs (see page 21), plus a bowl of cabbage and radish (see page 24) and some fried wontons.

60 g fermented red bean curd, mashed
3 cloves garlic, finely chopped
70 ml light soy sauce
100 ml Shaoxing wine
60 g hoisin sauce
60 g caster sugar
1 kg pork neck, cut lengthways into 4 cm wide strips
250 g honey

Whisk together the bean curd, garlic, soy sauce, Shaoxing wine, hoisin sauce and sugar until the sugar has dissolved. Add the pork and toss to coat well, then leave to marinate for 2 hours.

Preheat the oven to 240°C. Set a wire rack over a roasting tin with about a 3 cm depth of water added. Place the marinated pork directly onto the rack and roast for 30 minutes or until well caramelised and quite dark in places.

Warm the honey in a small heavy-based saucepan over low heat, then brush all over the pork strips and leave to cool. Cut into slices just before serving.

GUANGXI-STYLE CRISPY PORK BELLY WITH CORIANDER, PEANUTS, RED ONION AND SESAME SEEDS

Serves 4–6 as part of a shared meal

At a Guangxi restaurant in Beijing, I was struck by how many of the dishes were served with fresh herbs and vegetables. They reminded me of Thai salads – there was even the hot, sour and salty thing going on. This crispy pork salad was inspired by a few of those Guangxi dishes, and it has proved to be one of the most popular on the menu.

250 g crispy pork belly (see page 21)
½ small red onion, finely sliced
large handful of roughly chopped coriander leaves and stems
handful of unsalted peanuts, roasted and crushed
1 tablespoon roasted sesame seeds
½ spring onion, finely sliced
1½ tablespoons Chinkiang black vinegar
2 teaspoons peanut oil
sea salt

Cut the pork belly into 2 cm cubes. Place the rest of the ingredients in a bowl and toss together, then add the pork and mix through.

Pile up in the middle of a large plate and serve.

HOT, SWEET, SOUR AND NUMBING PORK

Serves 4–6 as part of a shared meal

To me, this classic Sichuanese dish is like a grown-up (and pepped-up!)
version of the sweet and sour pork I loved as a boy – something
I have a soft spot for to this day.

50 g (⅓ cup) plain flour
35 ml Shaoxing wine
1 egg
1½ tablespoons water
250 g pork loin, cut into 2 cm cubes
vegetable oil, for deep-frying
1½ tablespoons peanut oil
6 cm knob of ginger, finely chopped
2 cloves garlic, finely chopped
1 teaspoon chilli flakes
½ teaspoon roasted and ground Sichuan
pepper (see page 17)
50 g white sugar
1 tablespoon chilli oil
50 ml Chinkiang black vinegar
2 tablespoons Chinese chicken stock
(see page 17)
1 tablespoon light soy sauce
1 spring onion, cut on the diagonal
into fine julienne strips

In a medium-sized bowl, whisk together the flour, Shaoxing wine, egg and water to make a smooth batter. Add the pork and ensure it is well coated, then set aside for 10 minutes.

Heat the deep-frying oil to 180°C. Working in batches, carefully lower the batter-coated pork into the oil and deep-fry for 2 minutes or until the coating is crisp and the pork is just cooked through. Drain on paper towel.

Place a wok over high heat. When it is smoking hot, drizzle in the peanut oil and stir-fry the ginger, garlic, chilli flakes and half of the Sichuan pepper until fragrant. Add the sugar, chilli oil, vinegar, stock and soy sauce and simmer until reduced to a thickish sauce. Add the deep-fried pork to the wok, tossing to coat well.

Spoon onto a serving plate, sprinkle with the remaining Sichuan pepper and garnish with the spring onion.

HUNAN-STYLE PORK BELLY
WITH FRESH AND DRIED CHILLIES
AND MUSHROOM SOY SAUCE

Serves 4–6 as part of a shared meal

With dried chillies, fresh chilli and chilli oil, this dry-fried dish packs a punch.
Crisp yet tender cubes of deep-fried pork make it hard to resist, and it has become
one of Spice Temple's signature dishes.

BRAISED PORK BELLY

2 litres water
150 ml Shaoxing wine
20 g yellow rock sugar, crushed
10 cm knob of ginger, sliced
10 cloves garlic, crushed
handful of spring onion tops
60 g fine salt
1 × 400 g piece boneless pork belly

Place all the ingredients, except the pork, in a stockpot or large heavy-based saucepan and bring to the boil. Taste for seasoning and adjust accordingly. Lower the pork belly into the stock and simmer for 1½ hours, then remove and leave to cool slightly. Place the pork on a plate or tray lined with baking paper, place another piece of baking paper over the pork and another plate or tray on top of that. Weight with tins of food or similar to press the meat, then refrigerate overnight.

TO DEEP-FRY THE PORK BELLY

vegetable oil, for deep-frying

Cut the pork belly into 2 cm cubes. Heat the deep-frying oil to 180°C. Working in batches, deep-fry the pork for 5 minutes or until crisp and golden. Drain on paper towel.

TO FINISH

60 ml (¼ cup) peanut oil
40 g dried long red chillies
100 g snake beans, cut into 4 cm lengths
1 fresh long red chilli, finely sliced
1½ tablespoons mushroom soy sauce
1½ tablespoons chilli oil
60 ml (¼ cup) Chinese chicken stock
(see page 17)
50 g garlic chives, cut into 4 cm lengths

Place a wok over high heat. When it is smoking hot, drizzle in the peanut oil and briefly stir-fry the dried chillies – watch them closely, as they can quickly burn. Add the snake beans and fresh chilli and stir-fry until starting to soften. Add the rest of the ingredients, stirring to deglaze the wok, and simmer until the liquid has almost completely evaporated. Add the deep-fried pork to the wok and continue to cook until all the liquid has gone. Spoon onto a serving plate and serve immediately.

STIR-FRIED TWICE-COOKED PORK BELLY WITH LEEK AND SICHUAN BLACK BEANS

Serves 4–6 as part of a shared meal

This dish is hot! It's also one of my personal favourites: I love the contrast of the melt-in-your-mouth pork belly and the soft leeks with the fierce heat of the chillies and the saltiness of the black beans.

1 × 400 g piece boneless pork belly, about 10 cm wide
100 g ginger, sliced
2 litres water
60 g fine salt

TO PRESS THE PORK

Place the pork belly, ginger, water and salt in a heavy-based saucepan and bring to a simmer, then turn off the heat and leave the pork to cool in the liquid. Remove the pork and place on a plate or tray lined with baking paper, place another piece of baking paper over the pork and another plate or tray on top of that. Weight with tins of food or similar to press the meat, then refrigerate overnight.

The next day, cut the pork into slices about 8 cm long and 3 mm thick, like bacon rashers.

2 tablespoons peanut oil
2 cm knob of ginger, finely chopped
2 cloves garlic, finely chopped
1 teaspoon chilli flakes
1 tablespoon Sichuan black beans
½ fresh long red chilli, finely sliced
½ fresh long green chilli, finely sliced
1 small leek, finely sliced
30 g bean sprouts, trimmed
1½ tablespoons Shaoxing wine
1½ tablespoons Chinese chicken stock (see page 17), plus extra if needed
1 tablespoon light soy sauce
2 tablespoons white sugar
30 g garlic chives, cut into 3 cm lengths

TO FRY THE PORK

Place a wok over high heat. When it is smoking hot, drizzle in half the peanut oil and quickly stir-fry the pork until golden, then remove and set aside.

Add the remaining peanut oil to the wok and stir-fry the ginger and garlic until fragrant. Add the chilli flakes and briefly stir-fry, then add the black beans, red and green chillies, bean sprouts and the leek and cook until soft and wilted.

Pour in the Shaoxing wine, stirring to deglaze the wok, then add the stock, soy sauce, sugar and garlic chives. Return the pork to the wok and cook for a minute or two just to warm everything through. Add a little more chicken stock if it seems too dry.

2 teaspoons chilli oil
2 teaspoons sesame oil

TO FINISH

Finish with the chilli oil and sesame oil and serve immediately.

NANJING-STYLE BRAISED PORK HOCK
WITH BLACK VINEGAR TEA

Serves 4–6 as part of a shared meal

I first tried this dish at a Nanjing restaurant in the Perth suburb of Burswood,
of all places. I promptly fell in love with the meltingly tender pork meat, and the
spectacle of watching it being shredded from the hock and dressed with black
vinegar tea at the table.

1 × 400 g pork hock, deboned (ask your
butcher to do this), bones reserved
3 litres master stock (see page 18)

TO BRAISE THE PORK HOCK

Wrap the deboned pork hock tightly in muslin, tying it up with kitchen string so
it keeps its shape during cooking. Place the pork hock in a saucepan of cold water
and bring to the boil.

Preheat the oven to 160°C. Transfer the pork hock to a roasting tin or casserole
dish that will hold it and the stock snugly and pour over the stock. The meat should
be completely submerged – add more stock or water if needed. Cover tightly and
braise in the oven for 3–4 hours or until very tender. Leave to cool slightly, then
refrigerate in the stock overnight.

50 ml vegetable oil
1 large onion, roughly sliced
100 g ginger, sliced
200 g sweet bean paste
350 ml Shaoxing wine
1 litre Chinese chicken stock (see page 17)
150 ml light soy sauce

BROWN SAUCE

Preheat the oven to 180°C. Place the reserved pork bones in a roasting tin and
roast for 2 hours until well browned. Meanwhile, heat the vegetable oil in a heavy-
based saucepan over low heat and sweat the onion and ginger without letting them
colour. When the onion is soft, add the sweet bean paste and simmer for 1 minute,
then pour in the Shaoxing wine, stock and soy sauce, stirring to deglaze the pan.
Add the roasted pork bones, bring to a simmer and reduce by half, skimming
regularly. Strain the sauce into a clean pan that will hold the pork hock.

vegetable oil, for deep-frying

TO DEEP-FRY THE PORK HOCK

Unwrap the pork hock and trim if necessary. Heat the deep-frying oil to 180°C.
Carefully lower the pork hock into the oil and deep-fry for 3–4 minutes or until
golden, then drain on paper towel.

90 g caster sugar
160 ml (⅔ cup) Chinkiang black vinegar
80 ml (⅓ cup) light soy sauce

BLACK VINEGAR TEA

Place the sugar in a heavy-based saucepan over medium heat and cook to a light
caramel (160°C on a sugar thermometer). Carefully pour in the vinegar and soy
sauce – stand back, as it will spit and bubble vigorously – then reduce the heat to
low and simmer until the sugar has dissolved again. Pour into a serving jug.

handful of finely shredded coriander
1 fresh long red chilli, finely chopped
2 cm knob of ginger, finely chopped
2 spring onions, finely sliced

TO FINISH

Place the pork hock in the pan with the brown sauce and simmer until warmed
through. Transfer the pork to a serving bowl or platter and shred the meat using
two forks. Add 80 ml (⅓ cup) of the brown sauce, along with the coriander, chilli,
ginger and spring onion. Toss gently to mix everything together, then serve with
the jug of black vinegar tea.

CHAIRMAN MAO'S RED-BRAISED PORK

Serves 4–6 as part of a shared meal

Supposedly this classic Hunanese braised pork was Chairman Mao's favourite
dish, and one he liked to eat every day. Once you've tasted it, you might too!
The red-braising not only makes the pork meat and fat meltingly tender, but
also creates a full-flavoured sauce with a hint of chilli and a sweet finish. This
is simple, home-style cooking – truly easy to master and wonderful to eat.

1 × 400 g piece boneless pork belly
100 g ginger, sliced

TO PRESS THE PORK
Place the pork in a pan of cold water with the sliced ginger and bring to the boil,
then turn off the heat and leave the pork to cool in the liquid. Remove the pork
and place on a plate or tray lined with baking paper, place another piece of baking
paper over the pork and another plate or tray on top of that. Weight with tins of
food or similar to press the meat, then refrigerate overnight.

1 tablespoon vegetable oil
40 g dried long red chillies
350 ml Shaoxing wine
100 g yellow rock sugar, crushed
300 ml light soy sauce
5 star anise
5 cassia bark sticks
8 cm knob of ginger, finely chopped
1.5 litres Chinese chicken stock
(see page 17), as needed

RED-BRAISING THE PORK
Cut the pressed pork into 2 cm cubes. Place a heavy-based saucepan over medium
heat, add the vegetable oil and fry the chillies until fragrant. Add 50 ml of the
Shaoxing wine and the sugar, then simmer until the sugar has dissolved and you
have a light caramel. Arrest the cooking by adding the remainder of the Shaoxing
wine and the soy sauce, along with the star anise, cassia bark and finely chopped
ginger. Add the pork, then pour in enough stock to just cover. Turn the heat
down to low and simmer gently for 30–45 minutes or until the meat is tender.

2 tablespoons potato starch
100 ml water
30 g dried golden mushrooms,
soaked in water overnight
30 g dried drumstick mushrooms,
soaked in water overnight
30 g dried black fungi, soaked in
water overnight
2 spring onions, cut into 5 cm lengths
2 teaspoons sesame oil
2 teaspoons chilli oil

TO FINISH
Mix the potato starch with the water in a small bowl to make a slurry. Drain and
rinse the mushrooms and fungi, then add to the saucepan of pork, along with the
spring onion and about half of the slurry. Stir until the sauce thickens, then add
more of the slurry as needed, stirring until a light sauce consistency is achieved.
Drizzle with the sesame oil and chilli oil, then serve.

LAMB
AND BEEF

STIR-FRIED CUMIN LAMB

Serves 4–6 as part of a shared meal

These earthy flavours are typical of the Muslim-influenced food of Xinjiang, a vast region in China's north-west. Try serving this with steamed buns (made from the dough on page 36, but left unfilled) instead of rice.

60 ml (¼ cup) peanut oil
200 g boneless lamb shoulder, thinly sliced
1 onion, sliced
2 cloves garlic, finely sliced
40 g pickled green chillies (see page 15), finely chopped
40 g pickled mustard greens, finely chopped
2 teaspoons fermented red chillies (see page 15)
1 tablespoon white sugar
1½ tablespoons light soy sauce
50 ml Chinkiang black vinegar
1 tablespoon chilli oil
1 teaspoon cumin seeds, roasted and ground
a few coriander stems, cut into 4 cm lengths

Place a wok over high heat. When it is smoking hot, drizzle in half of the peanut oil and quickly stir-fry the lamb until it is browned, then remove and set aside.

Add the remaining peanut oil to the wok and stir-fry the onion and garlic until fragrant, then add all the rest of the ingredients, except the coriander stems.

Return the lamb to the wok and simmer until the sauce is glossy and reduced. Toss through the coriander stems, then spoon onto a plate and serve.

STIR-FRIED LAMB WITH CORIANDER AND CHILLI >

Serves 4–6 as part of a shared meal

I love the way coriander is used as a vegetable here, not just a garnish. This simple dish is really just lamb, coriander and chilli cooked with a few aromatics and seasonings, but together they are close to perfection. Serve with fermented red chillies (see page 15) and a sliced fresh green chilli to the side.

potato starch, for dusting
sea salt and freshly ground black pepper
200 g boneless lamb shoulder, cut into 2 cm pieces
vegetable oil, for deep-frying
50 ml peanut oil
4 cloves garlic, finely chopped
4 cm knob of ginger, finely chopped
1 fresh long green chilli, finely sliced into rounds on the diagonal
1 fresh long red chilli, finely sliced into rounds on the diagonal
2 spring onions, cut into 4 cm lengths
handful of coriander stems, cut into 4 cm lengths
1 stalk Chinese celery, cut into 4 cm lengths
2 teaspoons Shaoxing wine
3 teaspoons light soy sauce
1 tablespoon coriander leaves
3 teaspoons chilli oil
3 teaspoons sesame oil

Place the potato starch in a wide shallow bowl and season with salt and pepper. Dust the lamb pieces with the seasoned potato starch, letting them sit in the bowl for about a minute so they get a good coating of starch.

Heat the deep-frying oil to 180°C, then deep-fry the lamb for 2 minutes or until golden and cooked through. Drain on paper towel.

Place a wok over high heat. When it is smoking hot, drizzle in the peanut oil and stir-fry the garlic and ginger until fragrant. Add the chillies, spring onion, coriander stems and Chinese celery and stir-fry until tender. Pour in the Shaoxing wine and soy sauce, stirring to deglaze the wok, then add the lamb and cook for a further minute.

Spoon onto a plate and scatter over the coriander leaves, then drizzle with the chilli oil and sesame oil and serve.

STIR-FRIED GRASS-FED BEEF FILLET WITH WOK-BLISTERED PEPPERS AND BLACK BEANS

Serves 4–6 as part of a shared meal

Whenever I go to my favourite Hunanese restaurant in Sydney, Chairman Mao, I always order their stir-fried peppers with black bean sauce. I also love the version at Lung King Heen in Hong Kong, which is seasoned with chilli soy sauce, but I really love this dish with beef fillet – it works a treat.

1 × 250 g beef fillet, cut into 5 mm thick slices (5 cm diameter)
2 tablespoons light soy sauce
3 cm knob of ginger, roughly chopped
1 clove garlic, roughly chopped
1-2 spring onion tops, roughly chopped
1 tablespoon peanut oil
½ red bullhorn pepper, cut into 10 cm long pieces
½ green bullhorn pepper, cut into 10 cm long pieces
1 spring onion, cut into 5 cm lengths
2 teaspoons fermented black beans
1½ teaspoons white sugar
2 teaspoons Shaoxing wine
1 teaspoon dark soy sauce
60 ml (¼ cup) Chinese chicken stock (see page 17)

Place the beef in a bowl with the light soy sauce and leave to marinate for 5 minutes.

Using a mortar and pestle, pound the ginger, garlic and spring onion tops to make a fine paste.

Place a wok over high heat. When it is smoking hot, drizzle in a teaspoon of the oil and quickly stir-fry the bullhorn peppers until they start to blister, about 20 seconds. Remove and set aside.

Wipe the wok clean and place over medium heat. When it is hot, drizzle in another teaspoon of oil and, working in small batches, briefly sear the beef (reserving its soy sauce marinade) – you want to keep it quite rare. Remove and set aside.

Wipe out the wok again and return to medium heat. Add the remaining oil and stir-fry the ginger, garlic and spring onion paste until fragrant. Stir in the blistered bullhorn peppers, along with the spring onion lengths, black beans and sugar, then pour in the Shaoxing wine, stirring to deglaze the wok. Simmer to reduce the sauce a little, then add the reserved soy sauce marinade from the beef, together with the dark soy sauce and stock and bring to a simmer.

TO FINISH

1 teaspoon chilli oil
1 teaspoon sesame oil
coriander leaves, to garrnish

Finally, return the beef to the wok and fold through. Drizzle with the chilli oil and sesame oil, then spoon onto a plate. Garnish with the coriander and serve.

STIR-FRIED GRASS-FED BEEF FILLET WITH CUMIN AND FERMENTED CHILLIES

Serves 4–6 as part of a shared meal

Fermented chillies bring complexity of flavour to this cumin-infused stir-fry
that makes the most of a nice piece of beef.

potato starch, for dusting
sea salt and freshly ground black pepper
1 × 200 g beef fillet, cut into 3 cm × 1 cm strips
vegetable oil, for deep-frying
50 ml peanut oil
1 onion, cut in half, finely sliced
4 cloves garlic, finely chopped
4 cm knob of ginger, finely chopped
2 teaspoons cumin seeds, roasted and ground
1 teaspoon fermented red chillies (see page 15)
2 tablespoons Chinese chicken stock
(see page 17)
1 tablespoon light soy sauce
1½ tablespoons Chinkiang black vinegar
handful of garlic chives, cut into 3 cm lengths

Place the potato starch in a wide shallow bowl and season with salt and pepper, then dust the beef strips with the seasoned starch.

Heat the deep-frying oil to 180°C and deep-fry the beef for 2 minutes or until browned and medium-rare. Drain on paper towel.

Place a wok over high heat. When it is smoking hot, drizzle in the peanut oil and stir-fry the onion until it is starting to soften. Add the garlic and ginger and stir-fry until fragrant. Add the cumin and fermented chillies and stir-fry until fragrant. Pour in the stock, soy sauce and vinegar, stirring to deglaze the wok, then simmer until reduced to a light sauce consistency.

Add the beef and garlic chives to the wok and cook for a further minute, just to warm the beef and wilt the garlic chives.

TO FINISH
3 teaspoons chilli oil

Drizzle with chilli oil, spoon onto a plate and serve immediately.

GRASS-FED BEEF FILLET
IN FIRE WATER

Serves 4–6 as part of a shared meal

The fearsome-looking fire water has an extraordinary, deep roasted flavour
from the chilli- and Sichuan pepper-infused oil. Addictively hot and numbing,
it's not for the faint-hearted – but once you get a taste for it, there's no turning
back. This fiery Sichuanese dish needs lots of steamed rice to soak up the rich,
chilli-spiked juices.

1 × 250 g beef fillet, cut into 3 cm wide slices
3 teaspoons potato starch, plus
1–2 teaspoons extra
3 teaspoons Shaoxing wine
420 ml peanut oil
30 g dried long red chillies, crushed and seeds removed
100 g Sichuan peppercorns, crushed
3 stalks Chinese celery, cut into strips about 4 cm × 1 cm
1 spring onion, cut into 4 cm lengths
90 g chilli bean paste
1 tablespoon white sugar
500 ml (2 cups) Chinese chicken stock (see page 17)
1 tablespoon dark soy sauce
2 teaspoons light soy sauce
1 tablespoon water

In a bowl large enough to hold the beef, stir the potato starch into the Shaoxing
wine until smooth. Add the beef, mix well and set aside for a few minutes.

Place a heavy-based saucepan over low heat and pour in 400 ml of the oil.
Add the chillies and Sichuan peppercorns and warm gently for 5 minutes to infuse
the oil.

Place a wok over medium heat. When it is smoking hot, drizzle in the remaining
peanut oil and quickly stir-fry the celery and spring onion, just to soften slightly,
then transfer to a serving bowl. Add the chilli bean paste and sugar to the wok and
stir-fry until fragrant, then pour in the stock and both soy sauces, stirring to deglaze
the wok.

Mix the extra potato starch with the water in a small bowl to make a slurry.
Add the beef to the wok, along with about half of the slurry. Stir until the sauce
thickens, then add more of the slurry as needed, stirring to achieve a light
sauce consistency.

Transfer the beef mixture to the serving bowl with the celery and spring onion,
then carefully pour the hot infused oil over immediately before serving.

STIR-FRIED BRISKET WITH
LUCKY MONEY DUMPLINGS
AND CHILLI PASTE

Serves 4–6 as part of a shared meal

Made in the same way as gnocchi, these are our attempt to replicate some
dumplings we once had in a Xinjiang restaurant. We call them lucky money
because they're shaped a little like coins – it's drawing a long bow, I know,
but you'll forgive me when you discover how silky, chewy and plain delicious
this dish is.

LUCKY MONEY DUMPLINGS

2 large potatoes
about 500 g (3⅓ cups) plain flour,
plus extra for dusting
fine salt

Steam the potatoes over boiling water for 1 hour or until cooked through – test
by piercing with a wooden skewer. When they are just cool enough to handle, peel
and press through a mouli or fine sieve. Weigh the potato, then weigh out half this
amount of plain flour. Gently knead the flour into the potato until smooth, then
leave to rest for 30 minutes.

On a lightly floured bench, use your hands to shape the potato dough into logs
1.5 cm in diameter, then cut each log into 1 cm thick slices. Press each slice with
your thumb to create the 'lucky money'. Working in batches, cook the 'lucky
money' dumplings in a large heavy-based saucepan of boiling salted water for
3 minutes or until they float to the surface, then drain well.

STIR-FRIED BRISKET

1½ tablespoons peanut oil
2 cm knob of ginger, finely chopped
2 cloves garlic, finely chopped
1 teaspoon chilli flakes
50 g chilli bean paste
30 g caster sugar
1½ tablespoons Shaoxing wine
50 ml Chinese chicken stock (see page 17)
150 g red-braised brisket (see page 20),
cut into strips
1½ tablespoons light soy sauce

Place a wok over high heat. When it is smoking hot, add the peanut oil and stir-fry
the ginger and garlic until fragrant. Add the chilli flakes and chilli bean paste and
stir-fry until the oil begins to take on a deep red colour. Add the sugar, Shaoxing
wine and stock and bring to a simmer, then add the brisket and soy sauce and
stir-fry until the meat is warmed through.

TO SERVE

1 spring onion, finely sliced
1 fresh red chilli, finely sliced
2 teaspoons sesame oil
2 teaspoons chilli oil

Stir the cooked dumplings through the stir-fried brisket, then spoon onto a plate.
Finish with the spring onion, chilli, sesame oil and chilli oil and serve immediately.

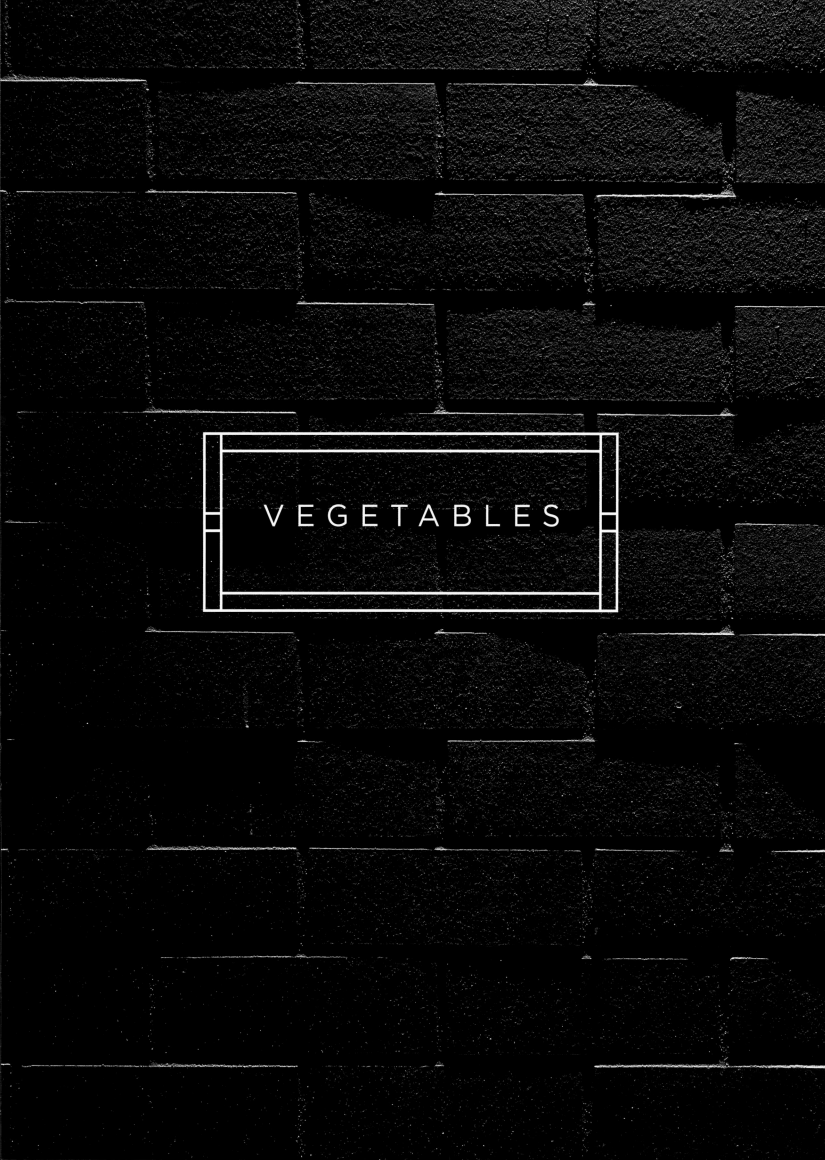

VEGETABLES

YUNNAN-STYLE HOT POT OF SHIITAKE, OYSTER, ENOKI AND WILD MUSHROOMS

Serves 4–6 as part of a shared meal

While we were dining at a Yunnan restaurant in Beijing, a hot pot of mushrooms and chilli with Yunnan ham was delivered to our table. We devoured every last bit of it, and wanted to find a way of including a braised mushroom dish on our menu, but one with a slightly less intense flavour. By using fresh instead of dried mushrooms and pulling out the ham to make it a vegetarian dish, we created a lighter-tasting version that's been a big hit.

2 tablespoons peanut oil
1.5 cm knob of ginger, finely chopped
2 small cloves garlic, finely chopped
⅓ cup (100 g) chilli bean paste
1 tablespoon Shaoxing wine
1½ tablespoons white sugar
2 teaspoons light soy sauce
500 ml (2 cups) Chinese chicken stock (see page 17)
200 g fresh shiitake mushrooms, stalks removed
200 g fresh oyster mushrooms
200 g fresh enoki mushrooms
100 g fresh black fungi, torn into large pieces
2 spring onions, cut into 5 cm lengths

Place a wok over high heat. When it is smoking hot, drizzle in the peanut oil and stir-fry the ginger and garlic until fragrant, then add the chilli bean paste and stir-fry briefly. Pour in the Shaoxing wine, stirring to deglaze the wok, then add the sugar, soy sauce and stock. Bring to the boil and taste for balance, adjusting with sugar and soy sauce as needed.

Add all the mushrooms, the fungi and the spring onion to the wok, reduce the heat to low and braise gently until the mushrooms and fungi are soft and the spring onion is just tender.

TO SERVE

30 g salted chillies (see page 15)

Garnish with the salted chillies and serve immediately.

GREENS STIR-FRIED WITH GARLIC

Serves 4–6 as part of a shared meal

Simple and delicious, this is all about the garlic and the wonderful taste and aroma of sesame oil. Use any greens you like here.

1½ tablespoons peanut oil
4 cloves garlic, finely chopped
500 g choy sum or mustard greens, cut into 8–10 cm lengths
handful of coriander stems, cut into 4 cm lengths
1½ tablespoons Chinese chicken stock (see page 17)
sea salt and freshly ground white pepper
1 tablespoon sesame oil

Place a wok over high heat. When it is smoking hot, drizzle in the peanut oil and stir-fry the garlic until fragrant. Add the choy sum, coriander stems and stock, then simmer until the liquid has almost evaporated. Season with salt and pepper and finish with the sesame oil, then serve.

GREENS STIR-FRIED WITH FERMENTED RED BEAN CURD

Serves 4–6 as part of a shared meal

This is a great way of cooking choy sum or fresh mustard greens – the fermented bean curd add a deep salty, savoury note. Asparagus also makes a lovely addition.

1½ tablespoons peanut oil
5 cloves garlic, finely chopped
500 g choy sum, cut into 10 cm lengths
handful of coriander stems, cut into
5 cm lengths
1½ tablespoons Chinese chicken stock
(see page 17)
2 tablespoons fermented red
bean curd, crushed
sea salt and freshly ground white pepper
1 tablespoon sesame oil

Place a wok over medium heat. When it is smoking hot, drizzle in the peanut oil and stir-fry the garlic until fragrant. Add the choy sum, coriander stems, stock and fermented bean curd and simmer until the greens are just tender and the liquid has almost completely evaporated.

Season with salt and pepper and drizzle over the sesame oil, then serve immediately.

STEAMED CHINESE BROCCOLI WITH OYSTER SAUCE

Serves 4–6 as part of a shared meal

Invariably, everyone who has eaten Chinese food has had this – it's a classic that demands the best oyster sauce. You can, of course, just buy a bottle of good-quality oyster sauce, but if you go to the trouble of making your own, it will make all the difference. This recipe makes about 1 litre and it will keep in the fridge for up to two weeks, ready to be used in stir-fries and with steamed fish.

---

50 g dried oysters, soaked in water overnight

60 ml (¼ cup) peanut oil

1 baby leek, roughly sliced

4 cm knob of ginger, sliced

50 g garlic, sliced

1 onion, roughly sliced

1 teaspoon sea salt

100 g caster sugar

100 ml Shaoxing wine, simmered until reduced by half

1 tablespoon potato starch

750 ml (3 cups) Chinese chicken stock (see page 17)

1 tablespoon dark soy sauce

2 tablespoons light soy sauce

HOUSE-MADE OYSTER SAUCE

Drain and roughly chop the oysters. Place a wok over medium heat. When it is smoking hot, pour in the oil and stir-fry the leek, ginger, garlic and onion with the salt until deep golden. Strain, reserving the vegetables and the oil separately. Wipe out the wok, then add the sugar and cook, stirring, until caramelised. Carefully pour in the reduced Shaoxing wine (take care as it will spit), stirring to deglaze the wok. Mix the potato starch with the stock in a small bowl until smooth, then add to the wok, along with both soy sauces. Return the leek, ginger, garlic and onion to the wok. Add the oysters, reduce the heat to low and braise very slowly for 2 hours. Leave to cool slightly, then blend in a blender at high speed and pass through a fine sieve. (Makes about 1 litre. Store in a sterilised glass jar or bottle in the fridge for up to 2 weeks.)

1.5 litres cold water

6 cm knob of ginger, bruised

3 teaspoons white sugar

1 tablespoon sea salt

500 g Chinese broccoli (gai lan), trimmed of any tough leaves and stem ends

STEAMED CHINESE BROCCOLI

Place the water, ginger, sugar and salt in a large heavy-based saucepan and bring to the boil over high heat. Add the Chinese broccoli, making sure it is completely immersed. When the water returns to the boil, cook for 2 minutes, uncovered. Drain, discarding the ginger, then cut the stalks of broccoli into bite-sized pieces and arrange on a plate. Drizzle with the oyster sauce and serve immediately.

STEAMED PUMPKIN WITH SICHUAN BLACK BEAN SAUCE

Serves 4–6 as part of a shared meal

Naturally sweet pumpkin is a perfect foil for this salty black bean sauce.

500 g pumpkin, peeled and cut into 3 cm chunks

STEAMED PUMPKIN

Steam the pumpkin in a steamer over simmering water for 35 minutes or until tender.

2 teaspoons vegetable oil
5 mm slice of ginger, finely chopped
½ clove garlic, finely chopped
50 g Sichuan black beans
3 teaspoons white sugar
1½ tablespoons Shaoxing wine
2 tablespoons Chinese chicken stock (see page 17)
1 teaspoon light soy sauce
1 teaspoon Chinkiang black vinegar
½ teaspoon sesame oil

SICHUAN BLACK BEAN SAUCE

Meanwhile, heat the vegetable oil in a heavy-based saucepan over medium heat and stir-fry the ginger and garlic until they start to colour. Add the black beans and stir-fry gently until aromatic. Add the sugar and Shaoxing wine and simmer until almost all the liquid has evaporated. Pour in the stock, soy sauce and vinegar and simmer until the black beans are tender and the sauce has thickened, then stir through the sesame oil.

½ spring onion, finely sliced
1 teaspoon chilli oil

TO SERVE

Drain the steamed pumpkin and place in a serving bowl. Dress with the Sichuan black bean sauce, then garnish with the spring onion and chilli oil.

SICHUAN-STYLE STIR-FRIED SPINACH

Serves 4–6 as part of a shared meal

Stir-fried spinach with garlic is a classic Cantonese vegetable dish, but Sichuanese cooks like to throw in some dried chillies to flavour the oil and add an extra dimension to the dish.

1½ tablespoons peanut oil
10 g dried long red chillies
4 cloves garlic, finely chopped
500 g baby spinach leaves
1 tablespoon Chinese chicken stock
(see page 17)
sea salt and freshly ground white pepper
1 tablespoon sesame oil

Place a wok over medium heat. When it is hot, drizzle in the peanut oil. Add the chillies and fry gently for a minute or so, just to flavour the oil. Add the garlic and stir-fry until it is just starting to colour, then add the spinach, stock, and salt and pepper. Stir-fry until the spinach has wilted, then finish with the sesame oil.

WILD BAMBOO PITH STIR-FRIED WITH SNOW PEAS, QUAIL EGGS, GINGER AND GARLIC

Serves 4–6 as part of a shared meal

The intriguingly named bamboo pith is actually a fungus that grows in bamboo forests, rather than anything to do with the bamboo plant itself. It is farmed, but the much more expensive wild bamboo pith has an infinitely better texture and a faint citrus flavour. Serve this as a dish in its own right, rather than a side. And if you can't get bamboo pith, try making it with fresh shiitake or oyster mushrooms – it will be quite a different dish, but still delicious.

50 g wild bamboo pith, soaked in water for 1 hour
4 quail eggs
1½ tablespoons peanut oil
4 cm knob of ginger, finely chopped
4 cloves garlic, finely chopped
100 g snow peas (mange-tout)
3 stalks Chinese celery, cut into 5 cm lengths
handful of coriander stems, cut into 5 cm lengths
1 tablespoon Shaoxing wine
1½ tablespoons Chinese chicken stock (see page 17)
sea salt and freshly ground white pepper
1 tablespoon coriander leaves
1 tablespoon sesame oil

Drain the wild bamboo pith, remove and discard the netting-like parts, then cut the stems in half.

Cook the quail eggs in a small saucepan of boiling water for 3 minutes, then cool under cold running water. Peel and cut in half lengthways.

Place a wok over high heat. When it is smoking hot, drizzle in the oil and stir-fry the ginger and garlic until fragrant. Add the snow peas, celery, coriander stems, Shaoxing wine and stock and bring to a simmer. Add the bamboo pith, season with salt and pepper and stir-fry for 2 minutes or until the bamboo is tender.

Transfer to a serving plate and finish with the quail eggs, coriander leaves and sesame oil.

STIR-FRIED MUSHROOMS WITH BLACK AND WHITE FUNGI

Serves 4–6 as part of a shared meal

This wonderful dish is a celebration of the diverse flavours and textures of fresh Asian mushrooms, so it's worth getting as many different varieties as you can find.

70 ml peanut oil
200 g fresh baby king brown mushrooms, sliced
20 g fresh oyster mushrooms, sliced
20 g fresh shiitake mushrooms, stems removed, caps sliced
20 g fresh shimeji mushrooms, sliced
sea salt and freshly ground white pepper
2 cm knob of ginger, finely chopped
2 cloves garlic, finely chopped
20 g fresh black fungi
20 g fresh white fungi
40 g fresh enoki mushrooms
3 teaspoons lemon juice

Place a wok over high heat. When it is hot, drizzle in the peanut oil and stir-fry the king brown mushrooms until lightly coloured. Add the oyster, shiitake and shimeji mushrooms, season with salt and pepper, and cook for 2 minutes. Add the ginger and garlic and stir-fry until fragrant, then carefully spoon off the excess oil from the wok.

Fold through the black and white fungi, enoki mushrooms and lemon juice.

TO FINISH

½ spring onion, finely sliced
pinch of roasted and ground Sichuan pepper
(see page 17)

Garnish with the spring onion and a pinch of Sichuan pepper, then serve.

COLD SHREDDED POTATO
WITH CHILLI DRESSING

Serves 4–6 as part of a shared meal

Cold shredded potato is something we came across in China at restaurants serving food from the south-central and south-western provinces of Hunan and Sichuan. At the time, we hadn't seen anything like it in Australia, and we really loved its crunchy, yet starchy texture.

SHREDDED POTATO

60 g potato, peeled and cut into fine julienne strips
1 tablespoon sea salt
25 g Lebanese (small) cucumber, cut into fine julienne strips
1 small spring onion, cut into fine julienne strips
handful of coriander leaves
1 teaspoon chilli flakes

Place the potato in a colander set over a plate and sprinkle over the salt. Mix well, then set aside for 15 minutes. Rinse the potato, then blanch in a saucepan of boiling water for 5 seconds, then refresh under cold running water. Drain well, then place in a bowl, together with the cucumber, spring onion, coriander and chilli flakes.

CHILLI DRESSING

50 ml vegetable oil
50 ml mushroom soy sauce
100 ml pickling liquid from pickled green chillies (see page 15)
70 g salted chillies (see page 15)
1 teaspoon sesame oil

Whisk the dressing ingredients together in a small bowl.

TO SERVE

Pour the dressing over the potato mixture, toss everything together and serve immediately.

STIR-FRIED LETTUCE WITH BACON AND XO SAUCE

Serves 4–6 as part of a shared meal

The sweet crunch of lettuce makes a perfect partner for the complexity
of XO sauce in this simple stir-fry.

50 ml peanut oil
20 g bacon, cut into fine strips
1.5 cm knob of ginger, finely chopped
2 small cloves garlic, finely chopped
1 baby cos lettuce, trimmed and
cut into 8 wedges
3 tablespoons XO sauce (see page 14)
1 tablespoon light soy sauce
2 teaspoons sesame oil

Place a wok over medium heat. When it is hot, drizzle in the peanut oil and
stir-fry the bacon until crisp. Add the ginger and garlic and stir-fry until fragrant,
then add the lettuce and lightly stir-fry until just wilted – it should still have some
crunch. Add the XO and soy sauces and simmer briefly to warm through.
Remove from the heat, then stir through the sesame oil, transfer to a serving plate
and serve immediately.

STEAMED KING ABALONE MUSHROOMS WITH GARLIC STEMS, CHIVES AND GINGER

Serves 4–6 as part of a shared meal

Also known as king oyster or French horn mushrooms, king abalone mushrooms are truly amazing. When sliced and steamed, they have the same texture as finely sliced abalone, hence the name. This is a dish you will cook more than once.

50 g garlic stems, cut into 5 cm lengths
50 g garlic chives, cut into 5 cm lengths
1 stalk Chinese celery, cut into 5 cm lengths
handful of coriander stems, cut into 5 cm lengths
2 cm knob of ginger, finely chopped
1 small spring onion, finely chopped
1 clove garlic, finely chopped
1 tablespoon Shaoxing wine
pinch of sea salt and freshly ground white pepper
100 g king abalone mushrooms
2 tablespoons vegetable oil

Mix all the ingredients, except the mushrooms and the vegetable oil, in a bowl, then transfer to a heatproof shallow bowl or lipped plate that will fit in your steamer.

Cut the mushrooms into 5 mm thick slices and arrange on top of the other ingredients, then steam over simmering water for 5–6 minutes or until the mushrooms are just tender.

Heat the vegetable oil in a small heavy-based saucepan until almost smoking, then carefully pour over the mushrooms and vegetables. Transfer to a serving plate and serve immediately.

PEAS STIR-FRIED WITH SOY BEANS, MUSTARD GREENS AND PORK BELLY

Serves 4–6 as part of a shared meal

Peas and bacon are a classic double-act in many cuisines – and with good reason.
This is fantastic with steamed rice, but I could happily eat a bowlful on its own.

50 g pressed pork belly (see page 20) or
unsmoked bacon
250 g baby peas
150 g fresh or frozen soy beans
fine salt
1½ tablespoons vegetable oil
2 cm knob of ginger, finely chopped
2 cloves garlic, finely chopped
1½ tablespoons Shaoxing wine
100 g pickled mustard greens, finely chopped
1 tablespoon white sugar
1½ tablespoons light soy sauce
100 ml Chinese chicken stock (see page 17)

Cut the pressed pork belly or bacon into slices 5 cm long and 5 mm thick.

Separately blanch the peas and soy beans in boiling salted water for a couple of minutes or until tender, then drain and set aside.

Place a wok over medium heat. When it is hot, drizzle in half of the vegetable oil and lightly stir-fry the ginger and garlic until fragrant. Pour in the Shaoxing wine, stirring to deglaze the wok, then add the mustard greens, sugar, soy sauce and stock and bring to a simmer. Add the peas and soy beans and cook until the sauce has reduced to a few tablespoons.

TO FINISH

5 mint leaves, roughly chopped
2 teaspoons sesame oil

Finish with the mint and sesame oil, then serve.

SNAKE BEANS STIR-FRIED WITH PORK AND XO SAUCE

Serves 4–6 as part of a shared meal

This famous and much-loved Sichuanese dish is taken up a notch by the addition of XO sauce, with its deep and complex flavour profile.

1½ tablespoons peanut oil
120 g pork mince
200 g snake beans, cut into 5 cm lengths
4 cm knob of ginger, finely chopped
4 cloves garlic, finely chopped
3 tablespoons XO sauce (see page 14)
2 tablespoons salted chillies (see page 15)
1½ tablespoons Shaoxing wine
100 ml Chinese chicken stock (see page 17)
25 ml light soy sauce
2 tablespoons white sugar

Place a wok over high heat. When it is smoking hot, drizzle in the oil and stir-fry the pork mince, stirring well to break up the meat. Add the snake beans and cook until their skin starts to blister, then add the ginger and garlic and stir-fry until golden. Add the XO sauce, salted chillies, Shaoxing wine, stock, soy sauce and sugar and simmer until the beans are tender.

TO FINISH

2 teaspoons sesame oil
2 teaspoons chilli oil

Finish with the sesame oil and chilli oil, then transfer to a serving bowl and serve immediately.

STIR-FRIED CABBAGE WITH BACON AND BLACK VINEGAR

Serves 4–6 as part of a shared meal

We love the combination of bacon and cabbage in any guise – but spiked with aged black vinegar, it's heaven. Textures matter in this dish, so take care not to overcook the cabbage. Pickles, such as the cabbage and radish on page 24 and cucumber on page 17 or 27, make a welcome addition to the table.

25 ml peanut oil
50 g Chinese ham, smoked bacon or speck, finely chopped
200 g Chinese cabbage (wombok), roughly chopped
1.5 cm knob of ginger, finely chopped
2 cloves garlic, finely chopped
½ teaspoon sea salt
2 teaspoons Shaoxing wine
1 teaspoon caster sugar
2 teaspoons light soy sauce
25 ml Chinkiang black vinegar

Place a wok over high heat. When it is smoking hot, drizzle in half of the peanut oil and stir-fry the ham or bacon until crisp, then add the cabbage and stir-fry until it begins to wilt. Remove and set aside.

Add the remaining oil to the wok and stir-fry the ginger and garlic with the salt until fragrant. Pour in the Shaoxing wine, stirring to deglaze the wok, then add the rest of the ingredients. Taste for seasoning and adjust as needed. Return the ham or bacon and cabbage to the wok and toss to combine well, then serve.

STIR-FRIED CORN WITH SMOKED PORK, CHIVES AND GARLIC OIL

Serves 4–6 as part of a shared meal

The sweet juiciness of corn goes perfectly with this smoked pork. A healthy dollop of Pixian chilli bean paste injects that vital burst of heat. If you don't want to smoke your own pork belly, speck or smoked bacon works well in this stir-fry.

GARLIC OIL

50 ml vegetable oil
3 cloves garlic, peeled

Gently warm the oil and garlic in a small saucepan to 80°C. Remove from the heat and leave to infuse for 2 hours, then strain.

SMOKED PORK BELLY

fine salt
100 g boneless pork belly
100 g tea-smoking mixture (see page 21)

Place the pork in a saucepan of cold salted water. Bring to a simmer and cook for 20 minutes, then remove from the heat and leave in the liquid to cool to room temperature. Drain well.

Make a shallow bowl from foil and place it in the base of a wok, then put the tea-smoking mixture inside. Set a wire rack over the top to hold the pork belly about 5 cm above the smoking mixture (if necessary, use some foil balls to elevate the rack) and cover tightly with a lid. Heat the smoking mixture in the wok over high heat until it starts to smoke, then briefly lift the lid off the wok and place the pork belly on the rack. Replace the lid and smoke the pork over high heat for 5 minutes, then turn off the heat and leave the pork to smoke for a further 3–7 minutes, depending on how intense you want the smoke flavour to be. Cut the smoked pork belly into 5 mm thick slices, like bacon rashers.

TO FINISH

1½ tablespoons peanut oil
4 heads of corn, kernels sliced from cob
2 tablespoons Pixian chilli bean paste
small handful of garlic chives, cut into 5 cm lengths
1 teaspoon caster sugar
1½ tablespoons light soy sauce

Place a wok over high heat. When it is smoking hot, drizzle in the oil and stir-fry the pork belly until golden, then add the corn and stir-fry until it is tender. Stir through the rest of the ingredients, then finish with the garlic oil.

DESSERTS

LYCHEE GRANITA WITH DRIED STRAWBERRIES AND HAZELNUT PRALINE

Serves 6

The praline can be made in advance and frozen in an airtight container for up to two months. You could serve this with fresh strawberries instead of dried.

LYCHEE GRANITA

60 g caster sugar
75 ml water
ice
500 g tinned lychees in syrup
juice of 1 lime, as needed

Place the sugar and water in a heavy-based saucepan over medium heat. Stir until the sugar has dissolved, then quickly cool down the syrup in an ice bath to ensure the fruit doesn't cook. Purée the lychees with their syrup in a blender until smooth, then add the sugar syrup. Add lime juice to taste, then transfer to an airtight container and freeze.

DRIED STRAWBERRIES

150 g strawberries, hulled

Thinly slice the strawberries using a mandoline or very sharp knife. Place in a dehydrator and leave until completely dried. Alternatively, spread out the strawberry slices on a baking tray lined with baking paper, then place in an oven with just the pilot light on and leave until completely dry, usually overnight.

HAZELNUT PRALINE

60 g liquid glucose
75 g (⅓ cup) caster sugar
60 g blanched hazelnuts, coarsely chopped

Preheat the oven to 160°C. Place the glucose in a wide shallow pan, such as a sauté pan, and place over low heat to melt. Add a third of the sugar and stir to dissolve, then repeat until all the sugar has been added. Increase the heat and cook the sugar syrup to a rich amber (175°C on a sugar thermometer), without stirring.

Meanwhile, spread the hazelnuts over a baking tray and roast for 6 minutes or until golden, then remove from the oven and keep warm. Clean the baking tray and line with baking paper.

When the sugar syrup is ready, add the hazelnuts and stir until completely coated. Remove the praline from the heat and pour it onto the lined baking tray. Leave to cool, then, using a mortar and pestle, break into small pieces.

TO SERVE

Scrape the granita with a fork to get a nice fluffy texture, then spoon into bowls. Scatter over the praline and dried strawberries and serve immediately.

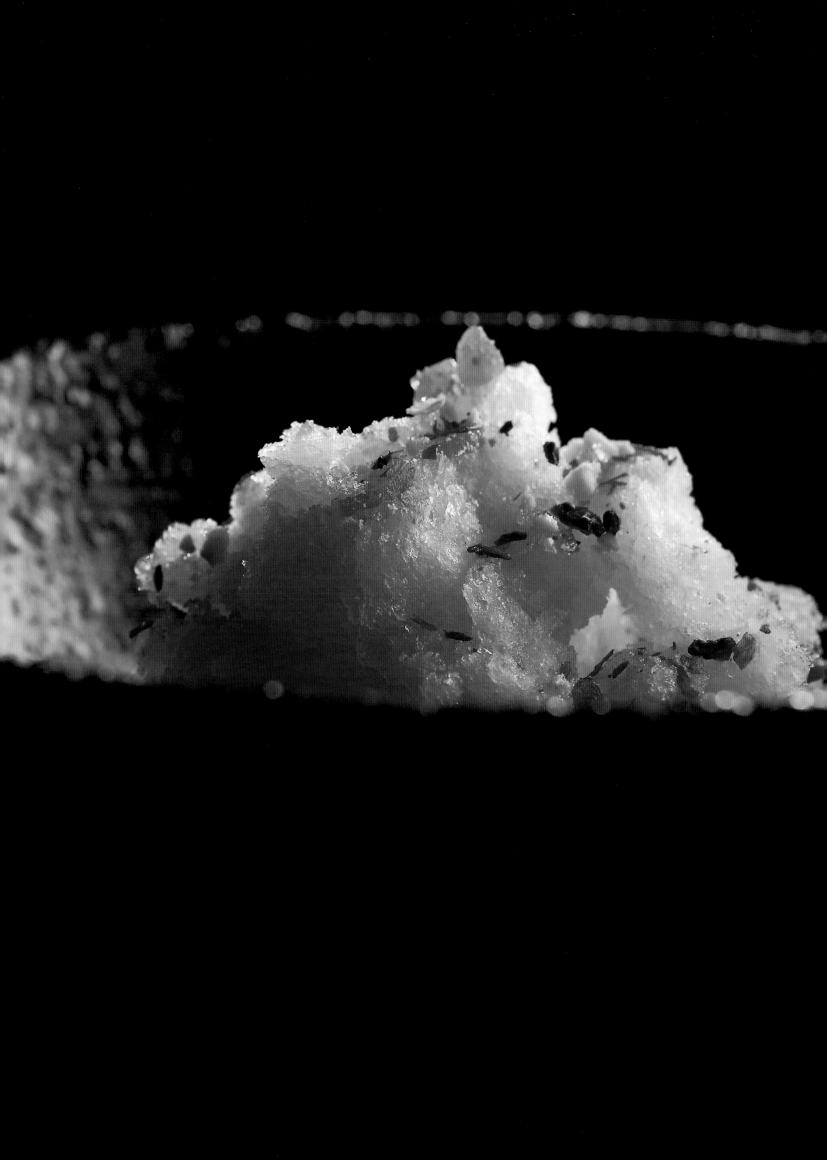

CARAMEL, CHOCOLATE AND PEANUT PARFAIT

Serves 6

As soon as pastry chef Catherine Adams put this on our first menu, we just knew it would become
a signature Spice Temple dessert – its sweet and salty notes make it the perfect way to finish a spicy
meal. Don't be put off by the length of the recipe: each component is very achievable, and then
all you need to do is put them together. Tanariva is a Valrhona single-origin milk chocolate from
Madagascar that has a wonderful balance, but any good-quality milk chocolate can be used.

275 g unsalted peanuts, blanched
310 g pure icing sugar
310 g egg whites (from about 8–9 eggs)
100 g caster sugar

PEANUT DACQUOISE

Preheat the oven to 180°C and line a 45 cm × 30 cm baking tray with baking
paper. Place the peanuts and icing sugar in a food processor and grind to a fine
flour-like powder. Whisk the egg whites to firm peaks, then gradually whisk in the
caster sugar to make a meringue. Gently fold in the peanut flour, then spread onto
the prepared baking tray and bake for 15 minutes or until golden. While the peanut
dacquoise is still hot, cut out rounds using an 8.5 cm round cutter, then leave to
cool – they will harden and become crisp.

230 g caster sugar
90 ml water
180 g egg yolks (from about 9–10 eggs)
200 g Valrhona Tanariva chocolate, or other
good-quality (33% cocoa) milk chocolate
50 g dark (53% cocoa) chocolate
475 ml pooring cream
¼ leaf titanium-strength gelatine, soaked
in cold water for 10 minutes

CHOCOLATE PARFAIT

Place 120 g of the sugar in a small heavy-based saucepan with the water and heat
to 115°C. Meanwhile, whisk the egg yolks in a heatproof bowl. When the syrup
reaches 115°C on a sugar thermometer, slowly pour it into the egg yolks, whisking
constantly. Keep whisking until the mixture has cooled to warm room temperature.
Melt all of the chocolate in a large heatproof bowl set over a pan of hot water,
taking care that the base of the bowl does not touch the water, then keep warm.
Heat 50 ml of the cream, then add the drained and squeezed-out gelatine leaf and
stir until it has dissolved. Whisk the remaining cream to soft peaks, then whisk in
the remaining sugar. Weigh out 225 g of the warm egg yolk mixture, then stir
in the dissolved gelatine mixture. Gently fold this mixture into the melted
chocolate, followed by the softly whipped cream.

160 g unsalted peanuts, blanched and
coarsely crushed
1 teaspoon sea salt
110 g (½ cup) caster sugar
1½ tablespoons water
110 ml pouring cream
oil spray, for greasing

PEANUT CARAMEL

Preheat the oven to 160°C. Place the peanuts on a baking tray and sprinkle over the
salt. Roast for about 10 minutes or until golden. Place the sugar in a small heavy-based
saucepan with the water and cook to a medium-dark caramel (180°C on a sugar
thermometer). Meanwhile, warm the cream in another small heavy-based saucepan.
Gradually add the warm cream to the caramel, stirring constantly, taking care as it may
spit. Stir the roasted peanuts through the caramel and cook for a minute more.

Line a baking tray with baking paper. Spray six 9 cm ring moulds with cooking
oil and place on the baking tray, then line each mould with a strip of baking paper.
Place 45 g of the warm peanut caramel in the centre of each mould and spread
out to form an even layer. Add 90 g of the chocolate parfait to each mould,
spreading it out evenly. Place a peanut dacquoise on top. Freeze the tray of parfaits
for 2–3 hours or until set.

100 g dark (53% cocoa) chocolate, chopped
30 g cocoa butter

CHOCOLATE DIP

Melt the chocolate in a heatproof bowl set over a saucepan of hot water, taking care
that the base of the bowl does not touch the water, then stir in the cocoa butter
until melted and combined.

TO FINISH

Remove the frozen parfaits from the moulds and dip half of each one into the
chocolate dip. Return to the tray and freeze until the chocolate has set. Remove
the parfaits from the freezer a few minutes before serving.

PINEAPPLE AND RUM GRANITA
WITH COCONUT PANNA COTTA

Serves 4

Fresh, light and delicious, this is a classic combination of tropical flavours.
Concentrate on getting the texture of the panna cotta just right, and let the
crunchy granita do the rest.

PINEAPPLE AND RUM GRANITA

50 g caster sugar
250 g fresh pineapple, chopped
150 ml water
1 tablespoon dark rum
1 teaspoon finely chopped mint leaves

Place the sugar in a heavy-based saucepan over medium heat until it melts and
caramelises. Keep cooking the caramel until it reaches 170°C on a sugar thermometer,
then carefully add the pineapple and water and simmer for 2 minutes. Remove
from the heat and leave to cool slightly, then blitz in a blender until smooth.
Transfer to a chinois or fine sieve set over a bowl and leave to drain slowly, without
pressing. Stir in the rum and mint, then place in a container and freeze for 4 hours
or until frozen.

COCONUT PANNA COTTA

125 ml (½ cup) coconut cream
240 ml pouring cream
40 g caster sugar
1 leaf titanium-strength gelatine, soaked
in cold water until soft
ice
125 ml (½ cup) double cream

Place the coconut cream, pouring cream and half of the sugar in a small heavy-
based saucepan over medium heat. Bring to the boil, stirring, then reduce the heat
and simmer gently for 1 minute. Add the drained and squeezed-out gelatine leaf,
along with the remaining sugar, and stir until dissolved. Sit the pan in a bowl of
iced water to cool it quickly, stirring constantly until it has a cream-like consistency.
Place the double cream in a bowl or jug, then add one-third of the coconut
mixture. Stir to incorporate, then pour back into the pan and mix well. Strain and
pour into four 125 ml (½ cup) dariole moulds. Refrigerate for 2 hours to set.

TO SERVE

200 g fresh pineapple, cut into 1 cm dice
50 g shaved coconut, toasted until golden
finely shredded mint leaves

Release the panna cotta by dipping the base of each mould into a bowl of hot water
for 10 seconds. Gently create an air pocket by pulling one side of the panna cotta
away from the mould, and carefully tip out the panna cotta. Place each
panna cotta in an individual serving bowl. Scrape the granita with a fork to get
a nice fluffy texture, then spoon around the panna cotta. Garnish with the pineapple,
coconut and mint and serve immediately.

MANGO MOUSSE WITH CONDENSED-MILK CHANTILLY

Serves 6

This is our homage to the Chinese mango puddings that do the rounds
on the yum cha trolley. Ours is a lighter, more elegant version, finished with
a translucent shard of sesame nougatine.

MANGO MOUSSE

1 ripe mango, flesh removed – you need
300 g mango flesh
125 g caster sugar
115 ml water
2 leaves titanium-strength gelatine,
soaked in iced water until soft
1½ teaspoons lime juice
ice
300 ml whipping cream

Purée the mango flesh in a blender or food processor, then transfer to a large bowl.

Place the sugar and water in a small heavy-based saucepan and bring to the boil, stirring to dissolve the sugar. Remove from the heat and add the drained and squeezed-out gelatine leaves, stirring until dissolved.

Stir the sugar syrup into the mango purée, along with the lime juice, then sit the bowl in a larger bowl of ice to cool the mixture quickly. When it is lukewarm (about 40°C), remove from the ice bath.

Whip the cream to soft peaks and fold into the purée. Pour the mousse into 6 individual serving glasses or bowls, then cover and leave to set in the fridge for at least 2 hours.

SESAME NOUGATINE

35 ml milk
100 g caster sugar
35 g liquid glucose
85 g butter
15 g plain flour
100 g sesame seeds

Preheat the oven to 160°C. Combine the milk, sugar, glucose and butter in a small heavy-based saucepan. Bring to the boil and cook until it reaches 106°C on a sugar thermometer. Remove from the heat and stir in the flour and sesame seeds. Pour onto a large sheet of baking paper, then cover with another sheet and roll out as thinly as possible, ideally about 1 mm. Bake for about 5 minutes or until golden, then leave to cool and harden before breaking into large shards.

CONDENSED-MILK CHANTILLY

100 ml condensed milk
180 ml (¾ cup) whipping cream
pinch of fine salt

Combine all the ingredients in a bowl and whisk to soft peaks.

TO SERVE

Spoon the chantilly evenly over the mousse and insert a shard of nougatine.

THREE-MILK CAKE WITH PISTACHIO AND RASPBERRY

Serves 12

This cake is inspired by those impossibly fluffy Cantonese sponge cakes that have been soaked in condensed milk. The combination of meringue and moist, rich sponge is a killer. We dared to take this off the menu once; however, after howls of protest from our regulars and staff, it was soon reinstated.

THREE-MILK CAKE

300 g (2 cups) plain flour
2 teaspoons baking powder
pinch of fine salt
6 eggs, separated
275 g (1¼ cups) caster sugar
125 ml (½ cup) milk
30 ml dark rum
1 teaspoon vanilla extract
375 ml (1½ cups) pouring cream
550 ml evaporated milk
500 ml (2 cups) condensed milk

Preheat the oven to 180°C and butter and flour a 30 cm × 20 cm Pyrex dish or cake tin. Sift together the flour, baking powder and salt, then set aside. In the bowl of an electric mixer, whisk the egg whites to stiff peaks, then whisk in the sugar. Add the egg yolks one at a time, ensuring each is well incorporated before adding the next. Alternately fold in spoonfuls of the milk and flour mixture, mixing to a smooth batter. Finally, fold in the rum and vanilla. Pour into the prepared dish or tin and bake for 30 minutes or until a skewer inserted in the centre comes out clean.

Remove the cake from the oven, but leave it in the dish. Use a skewer to prick the cake all over. Mix together the cream, evaporated milk and condensed milk, then pour over the cake. Leave to cool, then cover with cling film and refrigerate overnight.

MERINGUE

100 ml water
2 teaspoons lemon juice
300 g caster sugar
180 g egg whites (from about 4-5 eggs)
¾ teaspoon cream of tartar
2 teaspoons rose water

Place the water, lemon juice and all but 3 tablespoons of the sugar in a small non-reactive saucepan. Place over medium heat, stirring to dissolve the sugar. Cook the syrup without stirring until it reaches 120°C on a sugar thermometer.

Meanwhile, using an electric mixer, whisk the egg whites to stiff peaks, then whisk in the remaining sugar and the cream of tartar to make a meringue. With the mixer on low speed, slowly pour in a quarter of the sugar syrup and whisk to combine. Continue adding the syrup in this way, whisking well each time, until it is all incorporated, then add the rose water and whisk on medium speed for a few minutes until smooth and glossy.

THREE-MILK SAUCE

280 ml evaporated milk
240 ml condensed milk
140 ml pouring cream

Simply mix all the ingredients together in a bowl or jug.

TO SERVE

finely grated lime zest, roasted flaked almonds, roasted unsalted pistachios and fresh or freeze-dried raspberries, to serve

Cut the cake into 7 cm squares and place a square on each plate, then pour the sauce around the cake. Scoop a large spoonful of the meringue onto the top of each cake square and garnish with grated lime zest, flaked almonds, pistachios and raspberries.

CUSTARD BUNS

Makes about 25–30

A favourite yum cha dessert, these steamed buns generally come filled with either red dates or custard. Our version is stuffed with a luscious custard enriched with salted duck egg yolks. These are great served warm – I really like the contrasting textures. After steaming, the buns can be shallow-fried in a wok of hot oil for 90 seconds, then rolled in ground cinnamon mixed with caster sugar (see opposite).

CUSTARD

125 g butter, melted
50 g wheat starch
1 egg
200 ml coconut milk
125 g caster sugar
150 ml water
50 g custard powder
2 salted duck egg yolks

Combine all the ingredients in a bowl and blitz with a stick blender until smooth. Pour into a deep heatproof tray that fits inside your steamer, cover with cling film and steam over boiling water for 40 minutes or until just set. Use a spatula to scrape out the mixture into a bowl and blitz again until smooth.

BUN DOUGH

500 g (3⅓ cups) Hong Kong flour, plus extra for dusting
1 teaspoon caster sugar
1 teaspoon dried yeast
300 ml tepid water

Sift the flour into a bowl and mix in the sugar. Dissolve the yeast in the tepid water, then stir into the dry ingredients with a wooden spoon until a dough forms. Tip out the dough onto a floured bench and knead for 10 minutes or until smooth. Wrap the dough in cling film and leave to rest for 10 minutes.

TO SHAPE AND FILL THE BUNS

Unwrap the dough and punch lightly to knock it back, then knead for another 5 minutes or until smooth and elastic. Divide into golfball-sized balls, keeping them covered with cling film to prevent the dough drying out.

On a floured bench, roll out each ball into a round about 10 cm in diameter. Place 2 tablespoons of the custard in the middle, then bring the edges together and pleat the top to seal. Leave the buns, covered with cling film, in a nice warm spot to prove for 15 minutes or until slightly risen.

TO COOK THE CUSTARD BUNS

Working in batches, steam the buns in a single layer in a bamboo steamer over boiling water for 12 minutes or until fluffy.

PINEAPPLE AND RUM CHOCOLATE BAR

Makes about 20 bars

We created these little gems for diners who wanted to end their meal on
a sweet note without committing to much more food. Somehow, sharing dishes
Chinese-style often seems to result in a bit of over indulgence! These make
a really great finish to any meal.

NOUGATINE

40 g (½ cup) flaked almonds
150 g honey
100 ml pouring cream
40 g liquid glucose
80 g glacé pineapple, finely chopped
30 g crystallised ginger, finely chopped

Preheat the oven to 160°C. Spread out the almonds on a baking tray and roast for 8 minutes or until golden – keep an eye on them as they can quickly burn.

Line a 23 cm × 20 cm cake tin with baking paper. Place the honey, cream and glucose in a heavy-based saucepan and heat to 130°C on a sugar thermometer, stirring continuously. Remove from the heat and stir in the almonds, pineapple and ginger, then pour into the prepared tin, spreading it out evenly. Leave for 1 hour or until set.

RUM TRUFFLE

200 g dark (55% cocoa) chocolate, finely chopped
100 g milk chocolate, finely chopped
100 ml pouring cream
25 g liquid glucose
ice
20 g soft butter
45 ml dark rum

Place both chocolates in a heatproof bowl. Combine the cream and glucose in a small heavy-based saucepan and bring to the boil. Remove from the heat and leave to cool for a minute or so, then pour over the chocolate and stir to melt and emulsify. To avoid the mixture going above 34°C, place the bowl over a bowl of iced water. Gradually stir the butter into the chocolate mixture, then bring the temperature of the mixture down to between 25 and 32°C. Stir in the rum and pour into a deep baking tray. Cover with cling film and let it cool to 22°C, stirring once or twice as it cools, then pour onto the set nougatine and leave to cool to room temperature before refrigerating overnight to set. The next day, turn out onto a large sheet of baking paper, so that the nougatine is on top.

TO FINISH

cocoa powder

Cut into bars about 6 cm × 2 cm and store in the fridge for up to 30 days. When ready to serve, roll in cocoa powder, ensuring all surfaces are covered.

WHITE CHOCOLATE, BLACKCURRANT AND PEANUT CANDY BAR

Makes about 30–40 bars

With such a seductive combination of flavours, these sweet treats are worth making for any occasion. If you want to make these in advance, they can be kept in an airtight container in the fridge for up to 30 days. Just take them out half an hour before serving, so they're not too cold. Trimoline is an invert sugar syrup used in desserts in professional kitchens. Feuilletine are crispy wheat flakes used in professional kitchens to add a crunchy element to confectionary, ganaches, pastries and cakes. Both are available from specialty restaurant suppliers and food stores.

BLACKCURRANT JELLY

300 g frozen blackcurrant purée
135 ml fresh apple juice, strained
430 g caster sugar
10 g pectin
75 g liquid glucose
6 g citric acid

Line a 12 cm × 8 cm heatproof container with baking paper. Place the blackcurrant purée and apple juice in a stainless-steel saucepan and bring to the boil. Mix 40 g of the sugar with the pectin together and slowly sprinkle into the pan, whisking continuously to prevent lumps. Heat gently, stirring constantly until it comes to the boil. Gradually add the remaining sugar and the glucose, making sure each addition has dissolved before adding more. Bring to the boil and cook to 107°C on a sugar thermometer, then remove from the heat and stir in the citric acid. Skim off any froth, then pour into the prepared container and leave to set overnight at room temperature.

CRUNCHY PEANUT WHITE CHOCOLATE

120 g cocoa butter
770 g white chocolate
85 g trimoline
100 g peanut butter
500 g feuilletine
pinch of fine salt

Place the cocoa butter and white chocolate in a heatproof bowl and set over a pan of hot water to melt. Mix in the trimoline, followed by the peanut butter, then the feuilletine and salt. Pour the mixture onto the blackcurrant jelly, spreading it out evenly, then leave to set in the fridge for 1 hour.

TO FINISH

500 g white chocolate
100 g roasted unsalted peanuts, coarsely chopped

Cut the layered jelly and white chocolate mixture into bars about 6 cm × 2 cm. Melt the white chocolate in a heatproof bowl set over a saucepan of hot water. Carefully dip the candy bars into the melted chocolate, then sprinkle the peanuts on top before the chocolate sets.

PASSIONFRUIT MARSHMALLOWS

Makes about 30–40

These soft, sweet marshmallows, which have been served in my restaurants since
the 1990s, are hard to resist. I think it's something to do with their melting
texture and explosion of passionfruit flavour. Just a final word of warning:
these won't last long! Snow sugar is a mixture of icing sugar combined with
cornflour, used for dusting – you can't dust these with pure icing sugar as it would
dissolve straight away. It is available in supermarkets as icing sugar mixture.
These can be made ahead of time. Cut into squares and roll in snow sugar before
storing in an airtight container for up to one week.

135 ml strained fresh passionfruit juice
15 g powdered gelatine
375 g caster sugar
180 ml (¾ cup) water
50 g egg whites (from about 2 eggs)
tiny pinch of fine salt
snow sugar, for dusting

In a bowl, combine the passionfruit juice with the gelatine. Place the sugar and
water in a large heavy-based saucepan over low heat and stir to dissolve the sugar.
Once the sugar has dissolved, increase the heat and cook until the sugar syrup
reaches 125°C on a sugar thermometer. Remove from the heat and whisk in the
passionfruit juice mixture, making sure the gelatine is dissolved.

Place the egg whites and salt in the bowl of an electric mixer and start whisking
on medium speed. With the motor running, slowly pour the passionfruit syrup
into the egg white. Once all the syrup has been added, continue whisking on high
speed until the mixture has increased in volume and is thick and cool, gradually
decreasing the speed.

Pour onto a baking tray lined with baking paper and liberally dusted with snow
sugar; the marshmallow mixture should be 3 cm high. Spread out the marshmallow
evenly, then dust the top with snow sugar and leave at room temperature for
3 hours or until set.

Cut into cubes with a pizza wheel or sharp knife, then roll in extra snow sugar.

GLOSSARY

COOKING EQUIPMENT

To start cooking Chinese food, you need little more than a wok, a chopping board and a cleaver, all of which are inexpensive and readily available, but a few other tools and utensils make for more efficient preparation. If you find yourself making Chinese meals frequently, you might want to think about investing in a rice cooker, an electric wok and a deep-fryer – these appliances are good value these days, and will free up some space on your stove, which really helps when you're cooking multi-course shared meals.

WOK

This Chinese pan used for stir-frying, deep-frying, steaming, braising and smoking is amazingly versatile. A classic wok is usually made from thin carbon steel, which heats and cools quickly, giving you excellent temperature control whatever the cooking method. A wok is usually quite deep, meaning you'll need less oil for frying. The average wok for domestic use is about 33–36 centimetres in diameter.

Steel woks need to be seasoned before their first use. To do this, wash off the wok's protective coating with hot soapy water and dry it well, then pour in a little oil and heat it until it smokes. Turn off the heat and leave to cool, then reheat the oil four times. After the fourth time, leave the wok to cool and then, using paper towel, rub with some oil before storing. After each use, wash the wok in hot water and dry well (over heat is best), before rubbing it lightly with oil to prevent rusting. Don't wash your wok with soap, otherwise you'll need to season it again. Over time your wok will gain a wonderful patina and, importantly, food will not stick.

I've never really liked electric woks for stir-frying, although the newer models do at least get hot enough to do this effectively. The non-stick coating means that ingredients fall to the bottom easily, making it harder to get a nice crust on the food. What they *are* good for is steaming: you can place a bamboo steamer in an electric wok on the kitchen bench and it will give you more room on the stove. The other thing I like them for is braising – because of their shape, you can braise with less liquid, which concentrates the flavours nicely.

CHOPPING BOARD

Chinese cooks use a thick, round, whole slice of wood that is usually very heavy, allowing the cleaver to do its work. A standard chopping board can be used, however, the authentic article not only works much better, but also looks great in the kitchen. I find myself using one for most of my cutting needs.

CLEAVER

These come in various sizes. Those with thin blades are commonly used for chopping and shredding, while the larger, heavier cleavers are great for chopping poultry and slicing meat. The blade is easy to keep sharp with a sharpening steel or stone. A Chinese chef would use the blade for chopping, slicing and shredding, and the handle for crushing. The flat surface of the blade can also be used for crushing and for scooping ingredients from a board and transferring them to a pan or wok. Cleavers are very versatile and pleasing to use. Although all the cutting in this book can be done with Western-style knives, I do recommend learning to use a cleaver – all it takes is practice.

MANDOLINE

With its extremely sharp blade set into a wooden frame, a Japanese mandoline makes fine slicing and cutting into julienne much easier. Again, this is not essential, but something you will use often in the kitchen no matter what you are cutting. Handle with care!

MORTAR AND PESTLE

Essential for Asian cooking, a mortar and pestle is the one piece of equipment I would hate to live without. The weight of the pestle is used to help grind or pound ingredients like garlic, salt and pepper against the slightly rough surface of the mortar. Those made of stone seem to work the best for grinding pastes, and are readily available in Asian grocery stores.

BAMBOO STEAMERS

A stack of these inexpensive steamers is essential if you want to make your own dumplings. Larger ones are also invaluable for steaming fish, meat and vegetables.

CHINESE STRAINER

With its wire mesh and long bamboo handle, this is an excellent tool to have on hand when deep-frying. It makes it so much simpler to remove larger ingredients (chickens are a good example) from the hot oil, and allows them to drain before being set down on a cloth or paper towel. I also use one to remove food from boiling water. As a matter of fact, I use this for whatever style of food I'm cooking.

WOK SPOON

There are two main kinds of wok spoons: a flat fish-slice type used for lifting seafood out of woks or steamers; and a shovel-like spoon that allows you to stir ingredients and keep them moving, so they don't burn in the fierce heat of the wok. I suggest you make the small investment in both of these – they're cheap as chips and will make cooking easy.

INGREDIENTS

This section covers ingredients you can buy from Asian grocers, specialist food stores and some supermarkets. Recipes for homemade condiments, sauces and stocks are given in the 'Basic preparations', starting on page 14.

BEAN PASTES

Made with salted yellow or black beans, these impart body and flavour to stir-fries and stews. Sweet bean paste is a simple purée of spices and soy beans, with no chilli, and is often a by-product of the soy sauce production process. Chilli bean paste is a chunky paste with chilli flakes that has been fermented in earthenware jars in the sunlight, while a Sichuanese version, Pixian chilli bean paste, also includes fermented broad beans.

BLACK AND WHITE FUNGI

Both of these are often available fresh as well as dried from Asian grocers. As far as texture goes, the fresh versions are far superior to the dried equivalents: not only are they silky and crunchy at the same time, but they are also a good aid to digestion.

CASSIA BARK

Sometimes called 'false cinnamon' or 'Chinese cinnamon', cassia is the bark of the laurel tree or Indian bay, and is an important ingredient in Chinese master stocks.

CHILLIES

The fresh chillies used in this book are mostly of the long red or green variety. When it comes to dried chillies, most recipes call for the red, papery ones sold in large bags at Asian food stores, but some fiery dishes from the Sichuan and Hunan provinces use heaven-facing chillies. These dried cone-shaped, medium-hot chillies are so called because they grow upside down. When lightly fried in oil, they turn radiant red and lose some of their heat. Available from Asian food stores or online from alibaba.com.

CHILLI OIL

Made by steeping flakes of crushed dried red chillies in oil, chilli oil is great for adding some fire to dressings and stir-fries. Usually bright red in colour and sharp with heat, it is available from Asian grocers.

CHINESE SESAME SEED PASTE

Chinese sesame seed paste is made from roasted sesame seeds and is a lot richer and darker than the Middle Eastern tahini.

CHINKIANG BLACK VINEGAR

Made from glutinous rice and malt, this dark vinegar has a rich but mild flavour that grows more complex with age. We use Chinkiang black vinegar, which is named for the Chinese province where it is produced.

DRIED SCALLOPS ('CONPOY')

The earthy flavour of dried scallops, or 'conpoy', permeates XO sauces and also makes a luxurious addition to fried rice. Dried scallops can be found in Asian grocers – I prefer the larger Japanese ones to the smaller Chinese variety.

DRIED SHIITAKE MUSHROOMS

The texture and intense umami flavour of these dried mushrooms is unsurpassed. Dried shiitakes need to be rinsed and reconstituted by soaking in warm water for about 20 minutes, then draining; the stalks should always be removed as they remain hard and indigestible.

DRIED SHRIMP

These tiny dried shrimp should be a nice pinkish-red colour and quite soft. Don't buy brown or rock-hard dried shrimp – they will be stale and lacking in flavour. Before use, dried shrimp should be soaked in warm water for 20 minutes, then drained. They are good in stir-fries and are also used to make some chilli pastes and sauces.

DRUMSTICK MUSHROOMS

These mushrooms are indigenous to Yunan province. They can be purchased dried in packets from Asian food stores.

DUCK EGGS

Fresh duck eggs have a bluish tinge to their shells and can be stir-fried or used in omelettes. Salted eggs are generally steamed for 20 minutes before being used to garnish all sorts of dishes.

ENOKI MUSHROOMS

These slender, delicate mushrooms are delicious in salads, but are even better cooked for a few moments in a soup or as a garnish for stir-fries. They only keep for 3 or 4 days in the fridge, and should ideally be used very fresh.

FERMENTED BLACK BEANS

Fermented and preserved in salt, these small black beans come in packets that often recommend rinsing before use. I find the flavour more interesting and edgy if they're not rinsed, but added directly to braises and stir-fries.

FERMENTED RED BEAN CURD

This pungent ingredient is made from bean curd cubes that have been fermented until they have a very gamey aroma. It adds tremendous depth of flavour to dishes, but a little goes a long way.

FIVE-SPICE POWDER

Chinese five-spice powder is usually made from a mixture of cloves, cinnamon, star anise, fennel seeds and Sichuan peppercorns.

GOLDEN MUSHROOMS

These dried mushrooms hail from Yunan province and surrounding regions and can be purchased dried in packets from select Asian food stores.

HOISIN SAUCE

Hoisin is a thick, jam-like sauce made from soy beans. With a sweet, garlicky flavour that's deep and mysterious, it is generally used in stir-fries or as a dipping sauce for Peking or Sichuan duck.

HONG KONG FLOUR

Hong Kong flour is a highly bleached flour – a manufacturing process that not only whitens the flour, but also breaks down the gluten further and makes the flour softer. It has a similar protein level to pastry flour, which makes a good substitute.

LAOGANMA CHILLI CRISP SAUCE

This brand of chilli sauce contains dried chillies, soy beans and garlic. You should be able to find it in larger Asian supermarkets or online.

LAP CHEONG

Made from pork fat and meat, seasoned with Shaoxing wine, ground ginger and soy sauce, these air-dried Chinese sausages are used in stir-fries, fried rice and braises.

LAP YUK

This Chinese charcuterie product is made from pork belly seasoned with Shaoxing wine, salt and sugar. It is cured for 3 days, then smoked and steamed for 1 hour.

OYSTER MUSHROOMS

With their delicate flavour and pearl-like colours, these creamy mushrooms need only brief cooking.

OYSTER SAUCE

An all-purpose seasoning, this sauce works well with seafood, meat and vegetables. Look for varieties labelled 'oyster sauce', not 'oyster-flavoured sauce'.

PICKLED MUSTARD GREENS

Available at Chinese grocers, these pungent-tasting pickles are often added to stir-fries and braises.

POTATO STARCH

Extracted from potatoes, this starch is then dried and milled to a powder. It thickens sauces at a lower temperature and gives a much clearer result than cornflour.

PRAWNS

Remember to remove the dark vein (alimentary tract) to avoid grittiness in the finished dish. The easiest way to do this is to hook it out with a bamboo skewer. To butterfly prawns for quick and even cooking in a stir-fry, simply make a shallow cut along the back of each prawn.

PRESERVED EGGS

Preserved eggs are covered in a mixture of salt, lime and wood-ash paste and stored for about a month before using. During this time, the whites turn a clear, dark deep-green colour and the yolks become very creamy: just peel and serve with tofu or in rice porridge.

RED SHALLOTS

With a shape reminiscent of a garlic bulb, red shallots are very different from the small brown French shallot, and they have a mild flavour. When deep-fried (see page 21), they are often used to add a crisp texture and a sweet taste to dishes.

RED YEAST RICE (KOJI)

This reddish-purple fermented rice gets its colour from being cultivated with a mould, and is mostly used to colour foods and stocks. It is available from select Asian food stores.

RICE

I serve jasmine rice with all my Asian dishes – even noodles! The best way to cook rice is in an electric rice cooker, so if you cook a lot of Asian food it's a worthwhile investment. Don't salt rice when cooking it: the sauces of these dishes are salty enough and the accompanying rice should have a natural, neutral flavour.

SALTED CHINESE OLIVES

Preserved in brine and dried, this olive preparation imparts a completely different flavour from European-style olives.

SALTED RADISH

This is made by preserving daikon (long white radishes) in salt and then fermenting them. Rinsed and finely chopped, this is often added to fried rice or dumpling fillings.

SALTED YELLOW BEANS

These fermented soy beans have a complex salty, savoury flavour. Sold in bottles or jars, their consistency ranges from whole beans in brine to a thick sauce.

SESAME OIL

Sesame oil is one of the great flavours of China. Nutty and fragrant, a few drops added at the end of cooking give a nice lift.

SHAOXING WINE

This Chinese wine is made from glutinous rice fermented with water. It has a dark golden straw colour and a unique flavour. Shaoxing is widely available in Asian grocers and some supermarkets, but dry sherry is a popular and adequate substitute.

SICHUAN BLACK BEANS

Available in jars at larger Chinese supermarkets, this Sichuanese condiment is made from fermented black beans mixed with chilli oil, garlic and chilli flakes.

SICHUAN PEPPERCORNS

These are not really peppercorns at all, but dried small berries from the prickly ash shrub. Roasted and ground to make Sichuan pepper (see page 17), the spice has a wonderful numbing and warming effect. As Sichuan pepper and salt (see page 17), it is used as a condiment.

SOY SAUCES

Soy sauce is the fermented juice of soy beans and a staple of Chinese cooking. Light soy, usually labelled 'Superior Soy', is used for most cooking and is saltier than dark soy. Dark soy, labelled 'Soy Superior Sauce', is used mostly for braising. It is much stronger and maltier, with a thick, pouring consistency that contributes a rich, darker colour as well as flavour. Mushroom soy sauce is dark 'superior' soy sauce, flavoured with shiitake mushrooms.

SPRING ONIONS

Also known as scallions, shallots or green onions, spring onions are very common in Chinese cooking. Both the green tops and the white stems are used.

STAR ANISE

This eight-pointed seed pod is one of the most important components of five-spice powder, and a must for many Chinese stocks and braised dishes.

TANGERINE PEEL

This dried peel should be soaked in water before use (unless you need to grind it), and any remaining pith scraped off to remove bitterness. It is available in Asian grocers, but you can also dry strips of fresh zest from tangerines and mandarins in a low temperature oven for a similar result.

TIANJIN PRESERVED CABBAGE

Sold in tins or jars at Asian grocers, this regional speciality is made by pickling a local variety of cabbage with garlic and salt.

VINEGARS

At Spice Temple the vinegar I use most is Japanese rice wine vinegar, as it has a softer, less acidic taste than most European wine vinegars. Where a more complex flavour is required, I use Chinese Chinkiang black vinegar, which has a rich taste reminiscent of balsamic vinegar, although it is less sweet; Chinese red vinegar gives a more subtle flavour. White vinegar is also used to make some pickles and dressings.

WHEAT STARCH

Made by removing the protein from wheat flour, this fine powder is used to make the delicate dough for translucent dumplings.

YELLOW ROCK SUGAR

Available from Asian grocers, this crystallised mixture of sugar and honey is essential for red-braised dishes. Crush the larger crystals using a mortar and pestle before use.

ACKNOWLEDGEMENTS

Firstly, I would like to thank the dedicated Spice Temple kitchen and floor teams, past and present. It is because of their collective efforts that the Spice Temples are great restaurants. The memory of my amazing father started all of this, and I want to thank him for holding my hand and walking me down Dixon Street in Chinatown.

Thanks to my business partners, Trish Richards and Dave Doyle, who helped to make the dream of Spice Temple a reality. Andy Evans and Ben Pollard, for leading their kitchen teams with such great poise; and Sascha Richardson and Nick Beadle, for defining Spice Temple's hospitality and generosity on the floor. Thank you, Michael Clift, for all your help with the recipes. Andy and Ben, another pat on the back for that as well – it was truly a team effort. Richard Healey and Seb Crowther, nice chat on drinking booze with Chinese food – I really appreciate the discussion. Big thanks to Stephanie Young, my assistant, who doesn't have the easiest job in the world, as I have quite a complicated and busy (some may say crazy) life.

Thank you to Julie Gibbs, publisher extraordinaire. You make things very easy, and you focus on the most important thing: making me a beautiful book. Alison Cowan, thanks for your great editing – it makes me look like I speak English and can write with your studied input. Katrina O'Brien, Kathleen Gandy and Daniel New, thanks for all your work at Penguin and for the great design. Daniel, the book looks amazing. Deborah Kaloper, thanks for the clean and simple styling that reflects Spice Temple. Big, massive thanks to my mate Earl Carter – you don't take a half-bad snap, old boy. As usual, you captured the mood and feeling of not just the food, but the place. The spirit of Spice Temple lives in these pages. Thanks also for all the other wonderful things you have done for me in the past. Big kisses.

Lastly, to my family: we all love Spice Temple to pieces, and it is with great love that we put this book together, as we have all been part of it. Sam, my beautiful wife, and my amazing girls, Josephine, Macy and Indy, you are the most important things in the world to me. Never forget that I love you, and don't forget to look after me when I'm old. xxxx

INDEX

LANTERN

UK | USA | Canada | Ireland | Australia
India | New Zealand | South Africa | China

Penguin Books is part of the Penguin Random House group of companies
whose addresses can be found at global.penguinrandomhouse.com.

First published by Penguin Group (Australia), 2015

1 3 5 7 9 10 8 6 4 2

Design by Daniel New © Penguin Group (Australia)
Photography by Earl Carter
Styling by Deborah Kaloper
Typeset in Bembo by Post Pre-press Group, Brisbane, Queensland
Colour separation by Splitting Image Colour Studio, Clayton, Victoria
Printed and bound in China by 1010 Printing International Limited

National Library of Australia Cataloguing-in-Publication entry

Perry, Neil, 1957– author.
Spice Temple / Neil Perry; Earl Carter.
9781921384097 (hardback)
Includes index.
Spice Temple (Restaurant)
Cooking, Chinese.
Other Creators/Contributors: Carter, Earl, 1957– photographer.

641.5951

penguin.com.au/lantern